# STUDIES IN MURDER

*Herbert Fuller*

Showing the wheel and cabin window

# STUDIES IN MURDER

EDMUND LESTER PEARSON

With an Introduction by

ROGER LANE

OHIO STATE UNIVERSITY PRESS
*Columbus*

The reprinting of this book was made possible with the help of
The Ohio State University Libraries.



First Ohio State University Press edition published 1999.

Library of Congress Cataloging-in-Publication Data
Pearson, Edmund Lester, 1880–1937
Studies in murder / Edmund Lester Pearson : with an
introduction by Roger Lane.
p. cm.
Originally published: New York : Macmillan, 1924.
Includes bibliographical references.
ISBN 0-8142-0819-3 (cloth : alk. paper). —
ISBN 0-8142-5022-X (pbk. : alk. paper)
1. Murder—United States. I. Title.
HV6524.P4 1999
364.15′23′0973—dc21 98-50781
CIP

The paper used in this publication meets the minimum requirements of the
American National Standard for Information Sciences—Permanence of
Paper for Printed Library Materials. ANSI Z39.48–1992.
9 8 7 6 5 4 3 2 1

I met Murder on the way—
He had a mask like Castlereagh:
Very smooth he looked, yet grim;
Seven bloodhounds followed him:

All were fat; and well they might
Be in admirable plight,
For one by one, and two by two,
He tossed them human hearts to chew.

—*The Masque of Anarchy*

## CONTENTS

# INTRODUCTION

EDMUND Lester Pearson's *Studies in Murder* was originally published in 1924, during the golden era of American letters. A certified classic, it was first republished in a Modern Library edition just fourteen years later. Readers loved it; so did I, when I encountered it some time later as a young teenager, and for reasons that still hold. The five stories so compellingly told here are all examples of "true crime," one of the oldest, and certainly the most popular, of our literary genres. The first of them, "The Borden Case," a subject to which Pearson returned repeatedly throughout his career, is the classic account of America's classic murder mystery, a version that generations of writers have had to wrestle with ever since. It is clear from the opening pages that the author has great gifts, including a sense of history, or context, and a natural storyteller's eye for the telling detail. He is also opinionated, elitist, given to odd digressions and sometimes obscure literary and other references. But these characteristics are on balance more endearing than annoying, and in any case are all entwined with the lively, urbane, and ironic style of writing that is Edmund Pearson's hallmark, one that anticipated Truman Capote and Norman Mailer in bringing a touch of class to a form that needed it.

Accounts of murder and murderers date back in this country to the first century of British settlement. It was customary, in the seventeenth century, to condemn killers not only to die but to listen, during their final moments, to "execution sermons" delivered on the gallows. Puritan ministers seized these occasions as prime opportunities to save souls; drawing on the private confessions of the condemned, they sketched not only the crime that had led to the platform but the biography that had led to the crime, denouncing the corrupting influence of the contemporary equivalents of sex, drugs, and rock 'n' roll for the benefit both of those about to hang and of the throngs assembled to see them off. For those unfortunate enough to have missed the whole drama in person, the sermons were then published as pamphlets.

But if these printed accounts were intended to educate and to warn, they also had other and less uplifting effects on at least some of the young folks and servants who read them, and perhaps indeed their elders and betters. Crime fascinates as well as repels; among criminals the line between confession and boasting is a thin one, often crossed as the eighteenth century progressed. And not only convicted felons but publishers increasingly rebelled against the roles originally assigned them by earnest clergymen. It was discovered very early that sex and violence sold. As the eighteenth century gave way to the nineteenth, lithographs replaced woodcuts in the pamphlets that invariably followed—indeed anticipated—major executions, and ample bosoms joined dripping axes and mournful tombstones. Pious messages, too, gave way to lurid descriptions, as the words of the condemned crowded out the Word of God. One inevitable result of listening to these voices on the verge of the gallows was that "true crime" stories came sometimes to subvert rather than uphold the existing order, insisting that their subjects, especially if young, female, good-looking or well-educated, had been wrongly or even corruptly convicted. Virtually every murder involving middle-class principals, a hint of romance, or more than the usual amount of bloodshed was both "horrid" and "terrible" enough to inspire at least one illustrated pamphlet, perhaps a short book. Whether the innocent face depicted on the cover belonged to the victims or the accused, the account was always maudlin, extravagant, and breathless.

None of these last three adjectives could be applied to the work of Edmund Lester Pearson. Born in 1880, in Newburyport, Massachusetts, Pearson graduated from Harvard at the age of eighteen and embarked upon a career as a professional librarian. But he soon discovered that his real passion was for writing—at first a humorous, bookish column for the Boston *Transcript,* required reading for the codfish aristocracy of the era, later books and articles on a variety of subjects, from *The Believing Years,* an affectionate memoir of growing up along the Atlantic Coast (1911), to a boy's biography of Teddy Roosevelt (1920). A move to New York, in 1914, as editor of publications for the New York Public Library, placed him literally in the middle of the big city's literary life, a position from which he was able to contribute to such smart new publications as *The New Yorker* and *Vanity Fair.* But it was the closing chapter of one of his several works on books and book collecting, *Books in Black or Red,* published in 1923, which signaled a new direction for his career.

Chapter 12, "With Acknowledgements to Thomas De Quincy," was a rumination on that nineteenth-century author's famous essay entitled "Murder Considered as One of the Fine Arts." One apparent result of Pearson's survey of the field was his discovery that while a few Americans, notably Poe and Twain, had done estimable works of fiction, none of his countrymen had treated The Real Thing with the kind of distinction shown by several Scots and Englishmen. There was a niche here, he surely concluded; *Studies in Murder* filled it with panache the next year. The success of this turn to crime was great enough to allow Pearson, then at the height of his powers, to quit the library to write full-time. And while he continued to publish on a variety of other subjects, from *Queer Books* (1928) to *Dime Novels* (1929), his more important projects were *Murder at Smutty Nose,* released in 1927; *Five Murders, and a Final Note on the Borden Case,* in 1928; and *More Studies in Murder,* in 1936. *The Trial of Lizzie Borden,* finally, appeared in 1937, the year of his relatively untimely death, and solidified the reputation for which he was best known then and remembered now, as *the* American expert on famous homicides.[1]

---

[1] That is, among most of us; librarians are different. The most recent Pearson reprint appeared in 1976, when J. B. Durnell and N. D. Stevens affectionately edited some of his earliest work for the *Transcript* as *The Librarian: Selections from the Column of That Name* (Metuchen, N.J.: Scarecrow Press).

But even without the bio- and bibliographic guide just above, Pearson's writing is so idiosyncratically personal that a reader should be able to sketch his portrait from clues in the work itself. *Studies in Murder* alone shows us a rather conservative gentleman of middle years, a book lover of wide tastes, eager to share his own quirky interest in a variety of matters such as the controversy surrounding the proper swearing in of Jewish witnesses in the New York of 1870. The nostalgia for old New England is here, to balance the author's proud familiarity with contemporary Manhattan. So is his admiration for the bully values of Teddy Roosevelt, his staunch support for the death penalty, his contempt for the "childish minds" of those who read the Hearst papers and the "sob sisters" who pander to them. And here too, finally and not least, is his pointed sympathy, in the story of "Mate Bram!" for a motley crew of common sailors who, as poor men unable to raise bail, were under federal law condemned to months in a cold jail as material witnesses to a deadly crime at sea.

Few other readers will share my own early memories of *Studies in Murder,* the first of Pearson's true crime books (and the only one, unfortunately, in my mother's library). But as I look back on the experience of reading and rereading it, I think that "The Borden Case," in particular, had a real impact on my later career as a social historian. Like all of his stories, this one was chosen from out of the past, in this case from a time already receding in Pearson's day and even more remote from mine. One of the leitmotivs of his account is the "ghastly" morning meal shared by the several members of that doomed Fall

River household—several of whom had suffered or would suffer from nausea. To begin a steamy day in early August there was mutton, left over from some days before (in an era long before electric refrigeration was available), together with mutton soup, johnny cakes, coffee, and cookies. My own reaction, as a young and temporally parochial member of the mid-century American middle class, was first astonishment at the lack of fruit juice and cereal, followed by the dawning recognition that things were simply different back then—not only, and of course, in terms of the political dates in which we were all then drilled but in the homeliest of everyday matters. (Pearson himself had a rather different take on the same menu, part of his distaste for every aspect of life among the penurious late Victorian Bordens. All students of the crime have had to comment on the mildly puzzling behavior of the houseguest, Lizzie's Uncle John Vinicum Morse, who, on returning to Second Street from morning errands, stopped [innocently?] to sample some fruit from the backyard, somehow oblivious to the crowds already gathering around a house known to contain the bloody bodies of two victims of an ax murderer. Pearson notes drily that "perhaps Mr. Morse, as he thought of dinner, foresaw a recurrence of the mutton-soup and was fortifying himself against the blow, but in any event we should not begrudge him his pears, nor the two or three peaceful minutes he spent with them, before he went into the house.")

But if, as a contemporary of Lytton Strachey, Pearson shared the then-common reaction against the Victorianism of his own youth, he remained always a moralist.

There are many references, throughout his work, to "the admirable De Quincey" and to mystery fiction, a genre far more highly developed in his day than true crime. But despite his acute sense of craftsmanship and style, and his ability to treat the most solemn of matters with ironic humor, his interest in murder was by no means purely aesthetic and certainly not detached. There is no doubt, ever, of his own strict sense of justice. The five stories here all have quite different endings. One remains, to Pearson, as much a mystery as it was to the authorities who investigated it, while in another a miscarriage of justice was narrowly avoided. In the remaining three, his apparent judgments about those formally accused range from the fairly confident (although not, perhaps, beyond a "reasonable doubt") to the absolutely certain. But whatever his own verdict, he is always on the side of the victim or victims, fiercely indignant, even decades removed from an event, at those who found excuses for criminal behavior or allowed sentiment to trump reason in weighing the critical questions of guilt or innocence.

He remained, too, a Victorian in his treatment of sex and indeed of violence itself. We all recognize that a certain prurience about both underlies the appeal of much crime writing and reportage. And there is surely blood aplenty in *Studies in Murder:* an ax was the apparent weapon used in two of the five stories, involving in one case a pair of deaths, in another, three; two of the remaining victims were battered to death, a last one stabbed. But in one of his departures from earlier and less literate writers Pearson refuses to sensationalize;

the crimes are inherently "horrid" and "terrible" enough without the hackneyed adjectives, and they are described with no more than the detail necessary to set the scene or provide the clues. In both "Mate Bram!" and "The Hunting Knife," too, the possibility of a sexual motive, or of criminal sexual behavior, occurs to a modern reader almost as readily as it did to the tabloids of the day. But Pearson hardly acknowledges either. His restraint is especially evident in the latter case, in which the victim, a woman caught alone in her father's house, was found partially clad in the bedroom. When the alleged killer was put on trial, "Allusions were made to the possibility of a further motive, but no evidence was introduced charging the attempt or commission of any crime other than murder or robbery," and that in Pearson's account is the end of it. His appeal, to resort to a cliché that he himself would have abhorred, was to those who prefer the rapier to the bludgeon.

I am delighted, my old memories reinforced by a new exploration of this classic text, that contemporary readers are here given another chance to appreciate it. As a historian and teacher I might argue that Edmund Pearson's choice of five great stories, and the elegant way in which he tells them, add up to a most entertaining way to experience the Victorian age through its underside. But the simpler truth is that apart from any educational value the appeal of style, and fun, is timeless.

Roger Lane

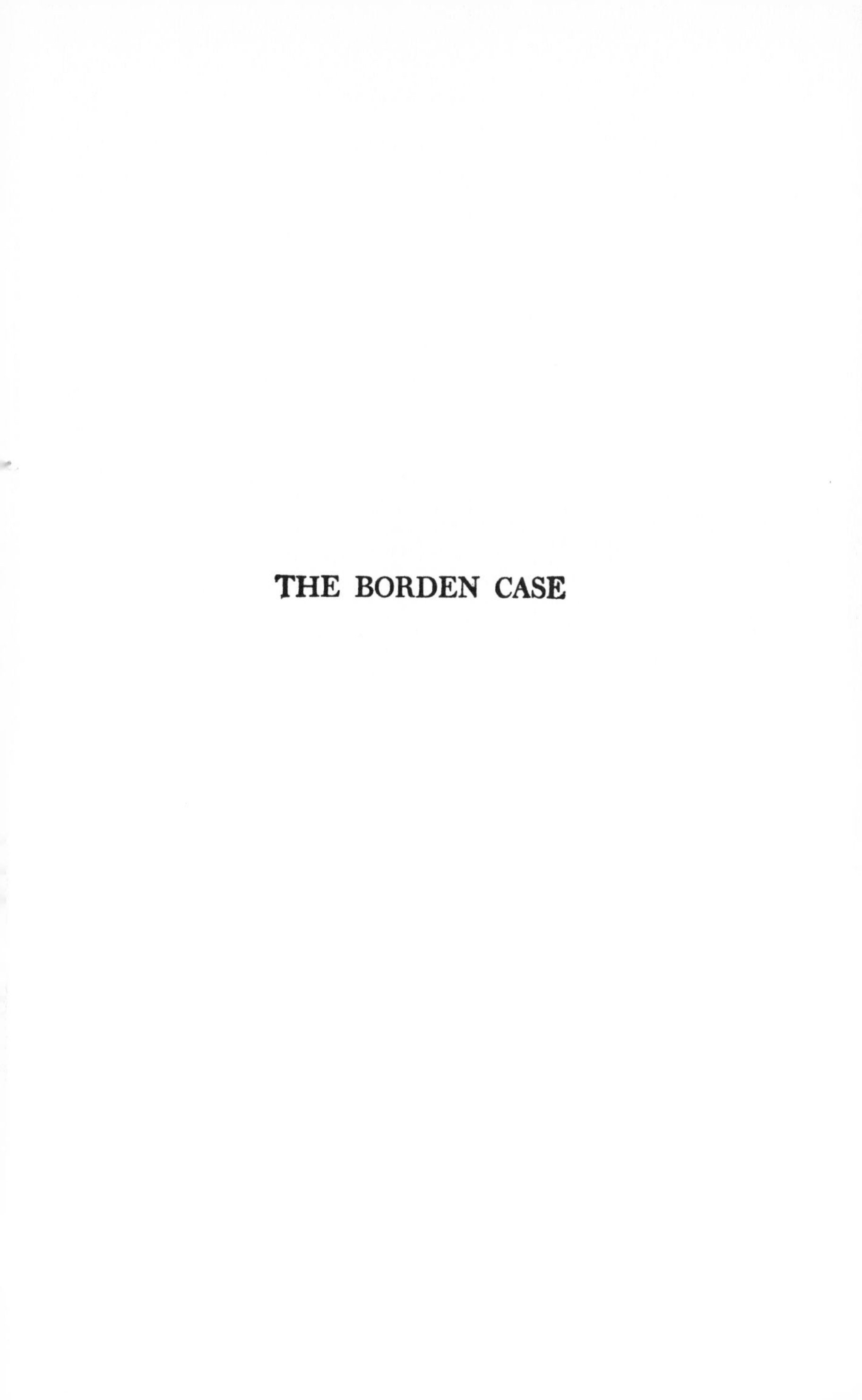

# THE BORDEN CASE

# STUDIES IN MURDER

## THE BORDEN CASE

THE Borden case is without parallel in the criminal history of America. It is the most interesting, and perhaps the most puzzling murder which has occurred in this country. There are in it all the elements which make such an event worth reading about, since, in the first place, it was a mysterious crime in a class of society where such deeds of violence are not only foreign, but usually wildly impossible. It was purely a problem in murder, not complicated by scandals of the kind which lead to the *crime passionel*, nor by any of the circumstances of the political assassination. The evidence was wholly circumstantial. The perpetrator of the double murder was protected by a series of chances which might not happen again in a thousand years. And, finally, the case attracted national attention, and divided public opinion, as no criminal prosecution has done since,—nor, to the best of my belief, as any murder trial in the United States had ever done before. People have become disputatious, even quarrelsome, over the probability of a verdict, one way or the other, over the justice of a verdict rendered, or over the wisdom of a commutation of sentence, in cases where was no doubt at all as to the identity of the slayer. In many celebrated cases the actual murder has been done openly and in public.

But during the investigation of the Borden mystery, and during the thirteen days of the trial, families throughout the United States were divided upon the question, and argued its points with a vehement interest for which no comparison suggests itself to me except the excitement in France over the Dreyfus case. And since there were no political and no racial matters at issue, there becomes apparent the extraordinary fascination of this case as a problem in human character and in human relations.

A murder may attract national attention for any one of a number of reasons. The actors may be persons of good position and respectability, as in the slaying of Dr. Parkman by Professor Webster, which amazed everybody in the days of our grand-parents, and is still discussed by English and foreign writers on criminology. Within our own time, those who follow the art of yellow journalism became agitated about that miserable affair in the Madison Square Garden in 1906. In this was no mystery whatever, and there would have been little interest except for the publicity of the crime, the scandals which attended it, and the fact that the victim was famous, and the other persons notorious. Otherwise, it was cheap and shabby; a carnival for the Sunday supplements. The warfare of gamblers, half a dozen years later, which came to a climax in front of the Hotel Metropole in New York, was really an incident in the history of municipal corruption; the killing of Rosenthal belongs in the class of crimes committed during feuds, rather than that of private murders. The lonely death of Mr. Elwell in his own home, was the subject of great interest; the opening chapter from a novel by Anna Katharine Green had been translated into reality. But it happened upon the verge of a world where such events are neither rare nor astonishing. More unusual was that scene upon the Phillips Farm in New Brunswick, upon whose horrors the discoverer casually wandered, as if stepping upon a stage laden with the dreadful quarry of an Elizabethan tragedy.

No one of these, I venture to assert, equals in peculiar interest the Borden murders in Fall River. Here were concerned neither gamblers, wasters, nor criminals, but quiet folk of a kind known to all of us. They were not members of a class among which killing is a matter of momentary impulse. They were so obscure that except for the event which put their names upon everybody's lips, we should never have heard of them. They became important in the light of what happened; the case was not like a play by a lazy dramatist who shirks his work of creation, and fills his scene with personages already famous. The crime itself—unexpected, hideous, unexplained—was the central point of interest. When the trial came to an end, ten months later, and the jury considered their verdict, there was before them, of course, only the task of answering, by yes or no, the question: was the accused person guilty? Apparently, they had little trouble in finding an answer to this, but the verdict did not clear up the astonishing puzzle. If, instead of a jury bound by our laws, they had been a committee of inquiry, charged with discovering an explanation of the crime, their task would have been as perplexing as anything which twelve men ever attempted. Each of the principal theories advanced at the time had its dark and doubtful points, and was moreover, as many reasonable men believed, in itself grossly improbable, and nearly contrary to human experience. Hardly ever was a murder committed where the limits of time and space so closed in upon the act, leaving such a narrow gap for the assassin to slip through to security.

The name Borden is found in all parts of the United States. It has been honorably associated with more than one important business, and in Canada two of the name have been eminent in politics. Many of the American Bordens are descendants of Richard or of John Borden who came from England in 1635-6 to live in Rhode Island. In that State, and even more in the adjoining county of Bristol, Massachusetts (which includes the cities of Fall River, New Bedford, and Taunton), the Bordens have always been numerous. The name has often been associated with that of Durfee. In 1778, when Fall River was attacked by a detachment of British troops, a Major Durfee led the citizens in a successful defence. Two of the houses burned during the fight were owned by men named Borden; one of these men was captured. In 1844, a Borden and a Durfee represented the district in the Legislature; and, in 1892, the year of the tragedy, these family names were borne by one or the other of the victims. Orin Fowler's "History of Fall River," in 1841, mentions the name Borden as second in frequency in the town. When the name came into painful notoriety in 1892, there were a hundred and twenty-five Bordens—representing, of course, many more than that—listed in the Fall River directory. It is illustrative of the frequency of the name that the indictment for murder, found in that year against a Borden, should have been attested by two others of the name, father and son, clerk and assistant clerk of the Superior Court, but not related to the accused person.

Fall River, like Dover or Calais, is one of those cities to which few go for its own sake, compared with the thousands who pass through on their way elsewhere. To the traveler into New England from New York or the South, it is associated with the name of a steamship line, and with an early morning change from boat to train. He looks around him, shudders, and hurries on. Reuben Paine, the hero of Mr. Kipling's "Rhyme of the Three Sealers," as he lay dying in the fogs of Bering Sea, let his mind travel far over the world to regret:

> No more I'll see the trawlers drift below the Bass Rock ground,
> Or watch the tall Fall steamer lights tear blazing up the Sound.

And if nobody except Reuben Paine, that I have heard of, ever referred to them as "Fall steamers," it is best to remember not only the exigencies of verse, but that the sight of the Fall River boats, from either shore of Long Island Sound at night, or from the water, is one that might well return to a man after many years. Current and local speech has not always been so respectful toward this steamship line, but Mr. Conrad Aiken has not hesitated to make one of the Sound steamers the scene of a poetical romance of much beauty.

The overwhelming importance of one industry, the manufacture of cotton goods, is perhaps what has prevented Fall River from becoming either interesting or attractive. It has its full complement of ugly streets, but of pleasant ones, fewer than such cities as Providence and Salem. Any American can see the town in his mind's eye, for there is a tedious similarity in places of this size; and the fact has been noted in the saying that West Newton, Massachusetts, extends all the way to the Pacific Coast. All have their Main Streets, under that name or another. Fall River has both the name and the thing itself. Thirty-two years ago there were perhaps a few more trees and a few less brick buildings upon it; the street-cars were not so noisy nor so many; the moving picture theatre, the automobile and the traffic policeman were still to arrive. Otherwise it looked nearly as it does to-day. The city had not then grown to have a hundred and twenty thousand inhabitants, but there were about seventy-five thousand, already including many of foreign birth, who were helping the native-born in their work, and sometimes perplexing them, and rendering them doubtful of the blessing of their presence. Citizens whose families had long been established in this country were inclined, as always, to suspect that any unusual offence was necessarily the deed of "some of those foreigners," forgetting the strange twists and distortions of which the oldest American stock has sometimes shown itself capable.

The newspapers of August, 1892, curiously prim and almost quaint to us to-day, contained small matter for excitement in that hot, dull season. There were speculations upon Mr. Cleveland's popularity; he was about to turn the tables on President Harrison, and defeat him in the November election. Mr. Gladstone's health was not too good. That aspiring sportsman, the Emperor Wilhelm, was racing his yacht at Cowes. John L. Sullivan was training for his last fight,—with Corbett. From the port of Palos had set forth a replica of the caravel *Santa Maria*, to take part in the celebration of the 400th anniversary of Columbus's discovery. Chicago was raising money for its World's Fair, and hoping that the cholera, reported in distant parts of Europe, was not coming as a guest. There were echoes of the Homestead strike and riot; Mr. Frick was recovering from the assault which had nearly ended his life. The *Teutonic* had broken the ocean record by crossing from Queenstown to New York in five days and eighteen hours. And the London police had caught a strange and terrible creature, named Neill Cream, and in great perplexity were uncovering a series of crimes, fiendish and inexplicable.

On the intensely hot morning of Thursday, August 4, 1892, something more than an hour before noon, an elderly gentleman named Andrew Jackson Borden was walking through South Main Street, Fall River. He was returning to his home which was only a few steps from the principal business street, and little more than around the corner from the City Hall, and the center of the town. It is probable that his mind was chiefly concerned with business, or with his family affairs, which were disconcerting. For the personages mentioned in the morning newspapers, and for the events described in them, it is fair to suppose he had no thought. So securely is the future hidden from us, that there is no way to imagine the astonishment which would have been his, could he have had any intimation not alone of the sufficiently startling fact that the remainder of his life time was then numbered by minutes, but that his name was to engage his countrymen's attention, for weeks and months to come, as if he were somebody of national importance.

However little he may have been known elsewhere, in his own town he was certainly not obscure. He was president of the Union Savings Bank, director in one or two other banks, and a director in various companies, including the Merchants Manufacturing Company, the Globe Yarn Mills, the B. M. C. Durfee Safe Deposit and Trust Company, and the Troy Cotton and Woolen Manufacturing Company. His business affairs had taken him on that morning to one or more of these banks. In his early life he had been an undertaker, and either that, or the gloomy custom of mankind, led him to dress in black, and in black clothes he trudged along on this tropically hot morning. His hair was white, for he was about seventy years of age, and he wore a fringe of white whiskers under his chin and along the angle of the jaw. His expression could be kindly, but it was stern; the thin lips—he wore no moustache—met in a way that denoted a stubborn character. The New England phrase is suggested: "He was as set as the everlasting hills of Zion." I have heard him described by one who remembers him coming from his farm,—a tall and erect old man, in his black clothes, carrying a little basket of eggs. That last bit is significant; Mr. Borden owned farms across the Taunton River, in addition to more than one house in the city. He had built one of the best business blocks in Fall River and the value of his estate was, during the trial, given as between $250,000 and $300,000. Yet he was not averse to bringing a few eggs to town, and selling them to some dealer. His manner of living had not changed as he rose from lesser things to greater, from one small business to financial power which, in that time and place, was not so different from that of a millionaire in a large city to-day. His was the melancholy lot of a man grown old in the treadmill of business, with no idea that life could be enjoyed, and no diversion except the further accumulation of money. Yet a just and honorable man, respected by everybody, and loved, perhaps, by one woman. He lived simply—many would say narrowly—in a small wooden house, number 92 (now 230) Second Street.

Mr. Borden had married twice. His first wife was a Miss Sarah J. Morse, by whom he had three children. After the death of the first Mrs. Borden, he married in 1865, Miss Abby Durfee Gray, who was six years younger than himself, and therefore in 1892 about sixty-four years old. With Mr. and Mrs. Borden there lived the two surviving daughters by the first marriage, Miss Emma L. Borden, about thirty-seven years old, and Miss Lizzie Andrew Borden, about thirty-two. These four persons, with a servant named Bridget Sullivan, made up the family at the Borden home.

On August 4th, however, Miss Emma Borden was

visiting some friends in Fairhaven, but the number in the house in Second Street remained the same, since John Vinnicum Morse, a brother of the first Mrs. Borden, had arrived the day before for a short visit. This was a man of sixty years, who lived in Dartmouth, Massachusetts. Visits to Fall River, and to the Borden house were frequent with him after his return to New England from twenty years spent as a farmer in Iowa. Serious and disturbing as the consequences of this visit were to Mr. Morse, it is almost impossible to regard his casual appearance in the household, on this occasion, without amused interest. Arriving, quite without baggage, on August 3rd, and solemnly pursuing for about twenty-four hours the objects of his visit,—which seem to have been calls upon other relatives and the inspection of Mr. Borden's farms—he found himself entangled in events of the most dreadful and sensational nature. The innocent bystander proverbially deserves our sympathy, but seldom gets it. Excepting young Mr. Monks, embarking upon the *Herbert Fuller*, for health, rest, and recreation (as recorded later in this book) it is hard to recall any figure similar to that of John Vinnicum Morse.

Mr. Borden continued through South Main Street, up Borden Street, and thence—it could have been only a few minutes walk, even for an elderly man—into Second Street. He arrived at his home at ten or fifteen minutes before eleven. He had some little difficulty getting admitted, going first to the side door and then to the front, (for it was a peculiar household as regards locks, bars, and bolts) but at last he entered. Within about twenty or thirty minutes a report came to the police that

Mr. Borden had died—by violence—and the investigation began.

Out of the mass of rumors and assertions, of charges and denials, it is necessary now to select certain facts which are generally admitted, and to trace the happenings of the week in Mr. Borden's home. It is useless to pretend that the family was either happy or contented. The presence in one home, of a step-mother and two daughters of mature years may be a fortunate combination with people of especially sunny disposition, but the Bordens seem to have been rather dour folk, to say the least. There was an aggrieved feeling about money on the part of the daughters, and this was of long standing. There was a perfectly comprehensible dissatisfaction with the manner of living, with the lack of such modern arrangements as a bath-room,—which some parents then considered new-fangled, expensive and unnecessary. When all these difficulties were discussed in court, the best that could be done was to admit some of them, but vigorously and not unreasonably to deny that they had any bearing on the murder, or that anything of importance could be deduced from them. But we have it, on the statement of a witness who was undisputed, that there was in the mind of that member of the family most concerned not to exaggerate the lack of harmony, a sense of impending disaster, and this only the night before the murder.

It had been a disturbing week. On Tuesday, August 2, Mr. and Mrs. Borden had been violently ill during the night. They were seized with vomiting. Miss Lizzie Borden said that she herself was affected, but not so as to cause vomiting. She went, she said, to the bedroom door of the older people, and asked if she could be of any help to them, but the offer was declined. Mr. Morse who came to the house after the family had eaten their dinner, at noon, on Wednesday, was served with that meal, which he ate alone. He ate again at breakfast on Thursday with Mr. and Mrs. Borden, but seems to have suffered no harm, nor was there any other return of this mysterious sickness, except that the servant Bridget Sullivan, was, alone of the household, sick on Thursday morning, the day of the murder, when she went into the backyard where she vomited her breakfast.

On Wednesday afternoon, after his dinner, Mr. Morse went to Swansea, to Mr. Borden's farm. He returned to the house on Second Street after eight o'clock, and sat talking with Mr. and Mrs. Borden. Miss Lizzie Borden was paying a call in a neighboring street, upon Miss Alice Russell, apparently one of her most intimate friends. During this call there was a remarkable conversation. Miss Borden said that she had decided to follow Miss Russell's advice, and go to Marion for a vacation. But she was apprehensive and depressed. She said: "I feel as if something was hanging over me that I cannot throw off." She described Mr. and Mrs. Borden's sickness, the night before, and expressed a suspicion that the milk might have been intentionally poisoned! Miss Russell was incredulous, and in this there is little cause for wonder. The suggestion that some person, with the tendencies of the Borgias, was, in the early hours of the morning, slipping deadly drugs into the milk can of a respectable family in a New England town is not one that ordinarily commends itself to the usual lady of good sense. The caller, however, went on to say that she feared her father had an enemy. He had trouble with somebody who came to see him. One man got into a quarrel with Mr. Borden and was ordered out of the house. Then there were robberies; the barn had been broken into twice. Miss Russell, who had formerly lived in a house next to the Bordens, and was still a not-distant neighbor, offered a more prosaic explanation of the barn robberies; they were merely boys coming after the pigeons. There had also been a daylight burglary, in the house, said Miss Borden. At one time or another in the conversation, this prophetess of disaster said that she slept in "fear that they will burn the house down over us." She was not precise as to who "they" were, but as everybody knows there are no more dangerous nor malicious beings in the world than "they." After a little more lugubrious chat of this kind, Miss Borden left her friend to her meditations. Like Cassandra's her forebodings fell upon doubting ears, but like Cassandra's her prophecies were by no means empty.

Miss Borden returned home, and although her uncle John Vinnicum Morse was seated in the room below, talking with her father and step-mother, and although she had not yet seen him, she did not pause nor speak to him. She went up-stairs to her own room. She was the last one to enter by the front door, which she locked. Bridget was the last to enter by the side-door, which she in turn locked. Mr. and Mrs. Borden that night as usual occupied their room in the rear of the second floor of the house; Miss Borden's room was next theirs. Mr. Morse slept in the guest-room at the front. The plan of the house makes clear the location of the rooms. Bridget's room was on the third floor. It is hard to conceive how any person other than these five could have been in the house, and I believe that no serious contention has ever been made that any stranger was concealed.

The next morning, Thursday, Bridget Sullivan came downstairs at a little after six o'clock, built a fire in the kitchen stove, and began to prepare breakfast. Mrs. Borden appeared about seven, and her husband and Mr. Morse soon following, the three breakfasted together. This breakfast was subsequently discussed at more than one legal investigation, so it may be said that according to Mr. Morse it consisted of mutton, bread, coffee, "sugar cakes" and bananas. The servant, who prepared the food, said that there was mutton-broth, as well as mutton itself, johnny cakes, coffee and cookies. Bridget insisted, in answer to the specific question, that to the best of her belief, they had no bananas that day. At all events, for a hot morning in mid-summer it was a breakfast well adapted to set the stage for a tragedy. One trembles at the thought of beginning a day in August with mutton-soup.

A lady said to me recently that, after more than thirty years, the details of the Borden case had vanished from her mind,—all except this awful breakfast.

Mr. Morse departed from the house at a quarter before eight. Mr. Borden let him out at the side door, and locked the screen door after him. A little later, Miss Borden came downstairs, and at first said to Bridget that she doubted if she cared for any breakfast. Finally,

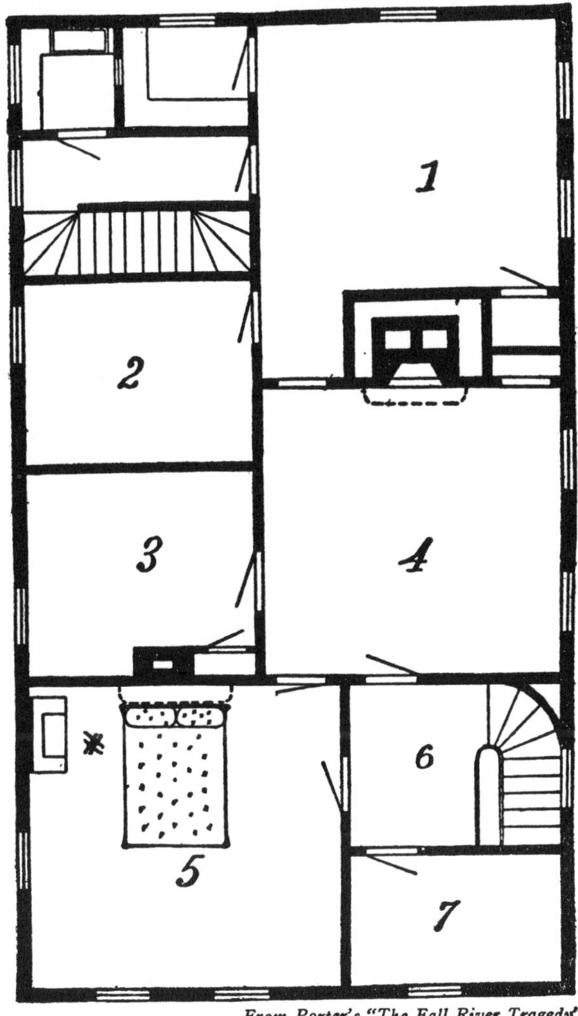


Second Floor, Borden House

1. Mr. and Mrs. Borden's bed room. 3. Miss Emma Borden's room. 4. Miss Lizzie Borden's room. 5. Guest room, where Mrs. Borden was murdered. 6. Hall or landing at head of stairs.

however, she decided to have coffee and cookies. Mr. and Mrs. Borden moved about the house; emptying slops and attending to other work of the kind, for Bridget was not expected to do this, nor was she even allowed in the rooms on the second floor. Soon afterwards, the servant was attacked by the sickness already referred to, and went into the yard, for perhaps ten or fifteen minutes, where she was relieved by vomiting. She described her illness as a "sick headache." When she returned to the house, Mr. Borden had gone downtown. This was between nine and half after the hour, and the three women were now, so far as anybody knows, alone in the house. Miss Borden was in the kitchen, still engaged, perhaps, with her cookies and coffee, while Mrs. Borden was wielding a feather-duster in the dining-room. The latter gave Bridget some orders for the morning; the windows on the lower floor were to be washed inside and out. A few minutes later, at about half-past nine, it would appear that Mrs. Borden, having made up the bed in the guest-room, came down-stairs again, and remarked that she was going back to put pillow-cases upon the two pillows of the bed in that room. She disappeared up stairs once more and no clear statement has ever been obtained from anybody as to whether she was again seen alive.

Bridget Sullivan went to the barn and to the cellar for brushes, pails, and other things for the window-washing. She came into the kitchen, the dining-room and the sitting-room to close the windows before beginning her work, and found those rooms empty. Neither Mrs. Borden nor Miss Borden was there. She began her duties outdoors and in, washing windows on both sides of the house. It occupied some time; she had a talk over the fence with "Mrs. Kelly's girl," and she made a number of trips to the barn for fresh pails of water. The Kellys were the next-door neighbors to the south.[1] Neighbors' houses were close to the Borden house on both sides, and in the rear. Finally Bridget finished outside, and was occupied indoors, when she heard Mr. Borden fumbling at the front door. He had already been at the side of the house where he found the wooden door open, but the screen door locked. Now he was trying his key at the front.

Bridget came from the sitting-room to let him in, but found the door not only locked, but triple-locked, with bolt, key, and spring lock. This is said to have been contrary to custom, and the slight annoyance caused her to make some exclamation, to say "Oh, pshaw!" At that moment she heard Miss Lizzie Borden at the head of the front stairs, or in the hall above, laugh. This little hall (6 on the plan) opens into Miss Lizzie Borden's room, and into the guest-room. Mr. Borden entered his house and went to the dining-room. His daughter came to him, asked about the mail, and said: "Mrs. Borden has gone out; she had a note from somebody who was sick." Mr. Borden took the key of his bed-room—it was a curiously well-guarded house—from a shelf, and went up the back-stairs, to his own chamber. He came down again very shortly, and sat by a window in the sitting-room. Bridget finished her window-cleaning, going from one

[1] The space between these houses is now (1924) closed by a brick building.

room to another. Miss Borden now appeared in the kitchen, to get an ironing board; this she took to the dining-room, and placing it on the table there, began to iron some handkerchiefs. All of this, from the entrance of Mr. Borden, occupied but a few moments.

Miss Borden then made an inquiry of Bridget, addressing her, according to her custom, as "Maggie," a name which had been inherited from a former servant.

"Maggie, are you going out this afternoon?"

"I don't know," replied Bridget, "I might and I might not; I don't feel very well."

Apparently nobody did feel very well in that house. Miss Borden had herself made a meagre breakfast, as we have seen. But the mutton-soup may account for that.

"If you go out," pursued the lady, "be sure and lock the door, for Mrs. Borden has gone out on a sick call, and I might go out, too."

"Miss Lizzie," Bridget asked, "who is sick?"

"I don't know," was the reply, "she had a note this morning; it must be in town."

And she went on ironing. Bridget rinsed the cloths she had been using, and hung them behind the kitchen stove. Miss Borden came into the kitchen, with another friendly bit of information.

"There is a cheap sale of dress goods at Sargent's this afternoon, at eight cents a yard."

Bridget said that the words used were possibly not "this afternoon" but "to-day." Bridget replied:

"I am going to have one," and went upstairs, up the back-stairs, of course, to her own room where she lay down on the bed for a rest.

Surprise has often been expressed at this action on the part of a servant, at eleven o'clock in the morning. But Bridget had been up since six, she had been working steadily and there was nothing more to be done until half-past eleven or twelve, when she was to get the mid-day dinner. It was her custom, if time allowed, to take such a rest; the Bordens were not unduly hard or exacting toward their servant. It has been seen that she had few of the duties of a house-maid, and none as chamber-maid. No astonishment could have been felt by any member of the family when she went upstairs. The dinner, moreover, was to be merely a repetition of the gruesome breakfast: "soup to warm over and cold mutton."

Shortly after she reached her room she heard the City Hall clock strike eleven. The house was quiet; she heard no doors opened nor shut, nor any other sound. She denied that she slept or even became drowsy; on second questioning she weakened the force of her denial a little, —she did not *think* that she slept at all. One rarely does know about this, and with many persons it seems to be considered a confession of breach of trust ever to admit closing the eyes, day or night. Second Street is a narrow street; wagons and carts probably rattled and rumbled past from time to time, but Bridget may well have failed to hear or to notice them. Nothing unusual was abroad in the house; nothing, at least, that came to the servant's ears, until some ten or fifteen minutes had passed. Then she heard Miss Borden's voice, and the tone of alarm was apparent at the first words.

"Maggie, come down!"

"What is the matter?" asked Bridget.

"Come down quick; Father's dead; somebody came in and killed him!"

Bridget descended instantly, and found Miss Borden standing near the side door. The servant started to enter the sitting-room, but was checked.

"Oh, Maggie, don't go in. I have got to have a doctor quick. Go over. I have got to have the doctor."

There was no doubt who was meant by this. Dr. Bowen, the family's friend and physician, who had already been consulted that week in regard to the strange illness, lived diagonally across the street, within a stone's throw. Bridget hurried to his house and reported the death to Mrs. Bowen, but learned that the doctor was, at the moment, not at home. She came back and told Miss Borden, and at the same time asked the question which was destined to be asked by everybody: "Miss Lizzie, where were you when this thing happened?"

The reply was: "I was out in the yard, and heard a groan, and came in and the screen door was wide open." Bridget was then ordered to go to Miss Russell's house and bring her. She departed again. In the meantime the going and coming of Bridget, pale and agitated, had attracted the attention of the nearest neighbor, Mrs. Churchill, who lived in the house to the north, hardly more than thirty feet away. No picture gives an accurate idea of the short space separating the two buildings. Mrs. Churchill went to the window, looked across at her neighbor's house, and saw the younger daughter of the family standing inside the screen door, and apparently excited or agitated. The distance was so slight as to make it possible to note that. She called to Miss Borden and asked her if there was any trouble.

"Oh, Mrs. Churchill," was the reply, "do come over. Some one has killed Father."

Mrs. Churchill hastened to her neighbor's house, went up the side-steps, and put her hand upon Miss Borden's arm.

"Oh, Lizzie! . . . Where is your father?"

"In the sitting-room."

"Where were you when it happened?"

"I went to the barn to get a piece of iron."

"Where is your mother?"

"I don't know; she had a note to go see someone who is sick, but I don't know but that she is killed too, for I thought I heard her come in . . . Father must have an enemy, for we have all been sick, and we think the milk has been poisoned."

Mrs. Churchill then learned that Dr. Bowen could not be found, and she volunteered to go out in search of another doctor. She crossed the street to a stable, and asked for help. Among the men who heard her was one named Cunningham, who telephoned to the police station. City Marshal Hilliard thus received the news at 11:15 and sent an officer to the house.

Mrs. Churchill returned to the Borden home, where in a few moments and before the arrival of the policeman, Bridget rejoined them, followed by Dr. Bowen. Then, for the first time, since the alarm was given, somebody entered the sitting-room. This was a small room, nearly square, with but two windows, both on the south side. The floor was covered with the usual garish,

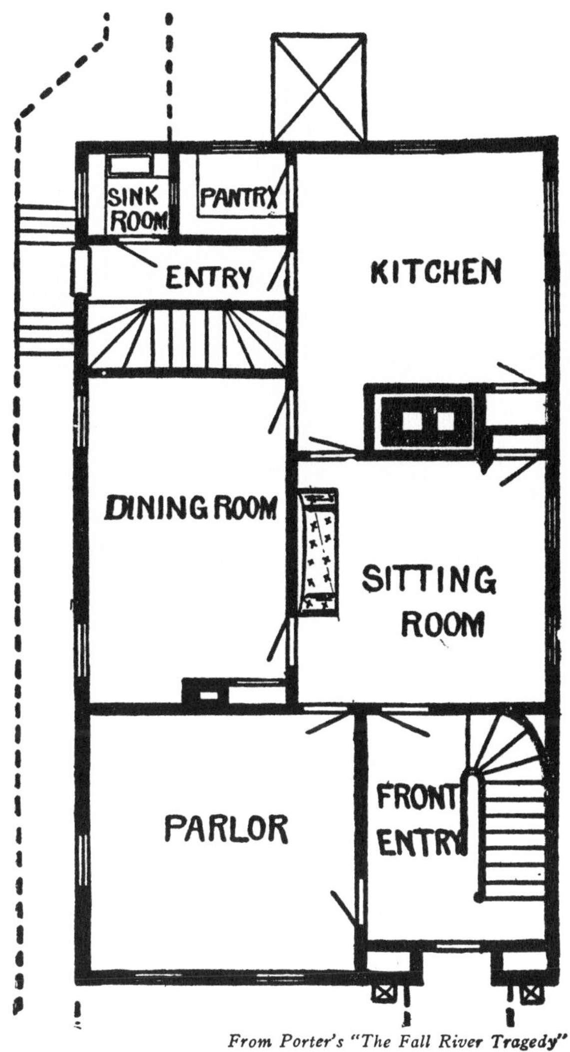


*From Porter's "The Fall River Tragedy"*

Ground Plan of the Borden House

Mr. Borden was killed on the couch in sitting room

flowered carpet, customary in such houses at that time, and the wall paper was of a similarly disturbing pattern. The furniture was mahogany or black walnut, upholstered with the invariable black horsehair. On the north side of the room, opposite the windows, was a large sofa, and on this lay the dead body of Mr. Borden with his head and face so hacked as to be unrecognizable even to his friend and physician, Dr. Bowen.

The doctor noticed that Mr. Borden had removed his coat, which was folded on the arm of the sofa, above the pillow on which his head rested. He had put on a cardigan jacket, in place of the coat. The body was stretched on the couch, but the legs from the knees down sloped toward the floor, and the feet rested on the carpet. It was his custom to take a nap in that position. Apparently, he had not altered his position after the attack. He wore congress shoes. There was no sign of a struggle; the fists were not clenched, and no furniture in the room was overturned. Dr. Bowen believed that he had been killed by the first blow, while asleep, but as to the other wounds which had been inflicted, in order to make death certain, he added: "Physician that I am, and accustomed to all kinds of horrible sights, it sickened me to look upon the dead man's face." Mr. Borden had been dead, so he thought, not more than twenty minutes.

Dr. Bowen asked for a sheet with which to cover the body, and then, at Miss Borden's request, went to send a telegram to her elder sister at Fairhaven. He was asked to break the sad news as gently as possible. Miss Russell had arrived by this time, and with Mrs. Churchill was engaged in the humane task of comforting Mr. Borden's afflicted daughter: fanning her, bathing her brows with cologne, and otherwise offering such help as would naturally be suggested. It was not observed that she asked for any of these feminine consolations, nor that she shed any tears, showed hysteria, nor betrayed great agitation. Indeed, it would not be too much to say that one gathers from the various accounts that she was, on the whole, as calm in her demeanor, perhaps calmer, than any of the women who fluttered about, and made unsuccessful attempts to "loosen her dress" and apply other forms of first aid. Grief shows itself in different ways in different temperaments; and it has often been noticed, even after natural deaths which have not come suddenly, that the person most bereaved does not, at once, exhibit the most sorrow.

Finally, Miss Borden said that she wished that somebody would try to find Mrs. Borden, as she thought she had heard her come in. Dr. Bowen had been sent for, and Miss Russell, and it now seemed appropriate to notify the person most concerned: the wife of the dead man. Bridget declined to go upstairs alone, but went with Mrs. Churchill from the kitchen to the front of the house, and up the front stairs. The neighbor said:

"As I went upstairs I turned my head to the left, and as I got up so that my eyes were on the level with the front hall, I could see across the front hall and across the floor of the spare room. At the far side on the north side of the room I saw something that looked like the form of a person."[2]

[2] Mrs. Churchill was looking through the door to the left of the figure 6 in the plan, and thence under the bed in room 5.

Bridget went into the room for an instant; Mrs. Churchill did not. They went down stairs again, hastily. When they had joined the others in the kitchen, Mrs. Churchill sank into a chair, with an exclamation or a groan. Miss Russell asked:

"Is there another?"

And Mrs. Churchill said: "Yes; she is up there."

The situation was quite beyond the experience of any woman; it is not surprising that Mrs. Churchill had no exclamation or remark in her vocabulary. Others went upstairs within a few minutes; Dr. Bowen was soon back at the house; and if the scene in the lower room was shocking, that in the upper was both ghastly and pitiful. The furnishing of the "spare room" would be homely and familiar to most of us. It had all the heaviness of the Victorian style of decoration: the carpet with gigantic clusters of impossible roses; the ponderous bed with carved head- and front-boards in some dark wood; and beyond, against the north wall, another ornate piece of furniture, a dressing table, or "bureau," with brass knobs and handles on the drawers, slabs of white marble on the top, ornaments and framed photographs, a lace-covered pin-cushion, and two white bottles or cruets, theoretically for scent or toilet water, precisely placed but purely ornamental, since nobody ever knew such receptacles to contain anything at all. The fringed bed-cover was smooth and clean, and the two pillows were covered by the white cases with ruffled borders which had been the last care of the poor woman who had gone to make up the bed which her guest had occupied.

On the floor between the dressing-table and the bed,

face-downward in a pool of blood, was the body of Mrs. Borden. Her head had been ferociously hacked and battered, like her husband's. But her wounds, unlike his, were not so fresh nor recent; the blood had ceased to flow from them, and that on the floor had coagulated; the temperature of her body was sensibly lower; she had been dead much longer than he. She wore a light dress of some cotton cloth. She was a short, heavy woman, weighing nearly two hundred pounds; how had she fallen at full length from an upright position without shaking the house, and alarming the others who were in it? Had she been caught by the assailant kneeling at the side of the bed to tuck in the bed clothes, and had there been, in consequence, no heavy fall? The position of the body, stretched out fully, with the arms under her, did not indicate this. If it were true, what evil fate was it that caused the two victims, the old man and his wife, she kneeling and he lying down, and both helpless, to be delivered thus into such savage and merciless hands?

The first policeman to arrive at the house was one named Allen. He was the committing officer at the police station, and happened to be there and available when the City Marshal (or chief of police) received the warning by telephone. He was dispatched to look into some "row" on Second Street, and may have thought that it was merely another "cutting affray" between some of "those foreigners." Certainly he did not know that he was to make the first report upon one of the most notorious and perplexing crimes which have ever engaged American police officers. It is one of the ironical circumstances of this case that upon the day when the Fall

River police were for the first and only time to be brought into national celebrity, and to start an investigation which was to call down upon themselves unlimited criticism and abuse—quite undeserved, as best I can judge—that upon this day of days in their history, more than half of them were away on their annual picnic at Rocky Point! Their chief was at his post, however, while a few members of the day force were on double duty.

Officer Allen stayed but a few moments at the Borden house. He looked upon the body of Mr. Borden, but at that time no discovery had been made of the other death, and he did not search the house. Instead of finding some fruit-vender, or vagrant, bleeding from one or two unimportant wounds acquired in a casual fight with a friend, he gazed upon the horrifying spectacle of a venerable and wealthy citizen barbarously murdered in his own home. A friendly writer says of Allen that he was, "to put it mildly, taken considerably aback by the sight in the house, and, to put it not too strongly, was frightened out of his wits. He left no guard upon the house when he ran back to the station" to inform the Marshal. It is, however, said that he stationed a private citizen at the side-door, with orders to admit nobody except the police and physicians. There have always been many to assert that a prompt and intelligent search of the house, with all that this implies, would have solved the mystery at once. This assertion seems to be based upon the knowledge gained after the fact and upon suppositions which may or may not be sound. It is not at all impossible that the police did, within twenty-four hours, discover nearly all the evidence which it was humanly possible to find. I think that it can even be put more strongly: it is probable that they did so. This statement holds true, it seems to me, whatever view one takes of the commission of the crime. If one follows the opinion of those who hold that the murders were the work of a stranger, an outsider, then this assassin certainly carried with him, when he fled from the house, all the most important evidence. And while it is not possible to discuss other theories, except as one may speculate upon a mystery, it is not unreasonable to believe that the most telling clews as to guilt were suppressed, destroyed or removed before the alarm was given. Officer Allen did not act with composure nor acumen,—but it may be that his omissions were less damaging than they have been considered.

What the police did not comprehend was that they were working in the dark against a person of considerable cunning and extraordinary audacity, who was moreover, protected by an incredible series of lucky chances.

Before a great number of people had arrived in or near the house, Mr. John Vinnicum Morse strolled down Second Street. He had been calling, at some distance, upon a nephew and niece, and now, as the dinner hour approached, returned to the Borden home, part of the way by street-car, but the rest of the way on foot. Although inside the house lay the murdered forms of his host and hostess, and although a small group of agitated persons had gathered in the kitchen, Mr. Morse was not aware of anything unusual. He went through the side yard, to the rear of the house, picked up two or three pears, and began to eat them. Pears enter this case more than once, and to all who are familiar with the region and the time of year, they suggest the atmosphere of an old New England garden in August. Perhaps Mr. Morse, as he thought of dinner, foresaw a recurrence of the mutton-soup and was fortifying himself against the blow, but in any event we should not begrudge him his pears, nor the two or three peaceful minutes he spent with them, before he went into the house. It was to be a long time before he was to know peace again, or to go mooning about Fall River and its vicinity upon his innocent errands. From a small expedition which he attempted, a day or two later, merely as far as the post-office, he returned with an escort of about one thousand people, and under police protection. Most unjustifiable suspicions were entertained against him for a number of days, but the police discovered promptly that his alibi was perfect, and that his account of his doings that morning was truthful and fully corroborated.

From shortly after mid-day it is impossible to think of Second Street as quiet, or of Number 92 as a house in which silence dwelt, as it had when Bridget heard the town clock strike the hour before noon. Crowds gathered in such numbers as to drive the newspaper reporters, in describing them, to the use of the phrase, "a surging mass of humanity." Friends, policemen, clergymen and doctors gathered in the yard, or swarmed through the house. The utmost pity was expressed for Miss Borden, since she had suffered a double sorrow through events far more distressing than natural deaths.

Dr. Dolan, one of the Medical Examiners for the county, had chanced to be passing the Borden house at 11.45, before the crowds had come. (Medical Examiner is the name in Massachusetts for the officer who elsewhere is called coroner. He is necessarily a physician.) Dr. Dolan entered the house, and with Dr. Bowen and others, viewed the dead persons. It was discovered that there had been no robbery from Mr. Borden's body: he wore a ring, and had in his pockets a watch and a pocket-book; in money there was $81.65. Dr. Dolan heard of the sickness in the family, two days earlier, and in consequence, took samples of the milk for analysis. He went with the police to the cellar, during their search of the house, and took note of some axes and hatchets which were found there. It was evident to all who saw the wounds in the skulls of the dead man and woman that these had been made by some heavy instrument, with a cutting edge,—without any doubt, a hatchet or something similar. During a visit, later in the afternoon, Dr. Dolan had the bodies photographed, and then removed the stomachs and sent them, with the samples of milk, to Edward S. Wood, professor of chemistry in the Harvard Medical School, and celebrated consultant in cases of legal medicine.

The search of the house proceeded; Miss Borden was questioned and questioned again by almost every officer who arrived. It was a distressing ordeal. One of those who had an interview with her was a patrolman, named Philip Harrington, who was afterwards described by the Chief Justice of the Superior Court as "intelligent." To him Miss Borden said that during the time of her absence from the house, when the attack upon her father took place, she was in the barn, that she was in there for twenty minutes. He expressed surprise that she did not hear anything from the house or the yard, sounds of the attack, of the opening or closing of doors, or of footsteps in the yard. She said that she was in the *loft* of the barn. This caused him still further surprise, since, as he and others afterwards discovered, the dusty loft of that barn, on a sultry August day, was about as uninviting a place as the steam-room of a Turkish bath. He and others made investigations as to the barn and the results of them will be considered later. Harrington asked her about any men who might have borne malice against her father, and she narrated one or two semi-angry conversations between her father and some strange man, which she had overheard. The policeman warned her about talking to anybody else, and suggested that it would be well for her to make no further statements for that day. Owing to the atrocity of the crime, he suggested, she might well be confused. She answered, however, with what he called "a stiff courtesy," and said:

"No, I can tell you all I know now, just as well as at any other time."

Mr. Edwin H. Porter, the historian of the Borden case, says that it was this conversation with Philip Harrington, as it was later reported to the City Marshal, which aroused suspicions "in the minds of the police that the daughter knew more of the circumstances of the tragedy than she cared to tell." The police were to pay dearly for such suspicions, but it seems hard to understand, in view of what has been related, to say nothing of what was yet to be discovered, how they could have avoided them. And yet it was a monstrous thing to suspect. As time went on, it took the form not of a mere accusation of complicity, or guilty knowledge of the crime, but of the part of principal and sole actor in it. And to suggest that a woman of good family, of blameless life and hitherto unimpeachable character, could possibly commit two such murders, is to suggest something so rare as to be almost unknown to criminology. It is beside the question to cite the many homicides of which women have been proven guilty. Nearly always, when the victim was an adult person, they have been murders by poison or by shooting. When, in modern times, the attack has taken a more brutal form, the murderess has usually been a woman of base antecedents, one from the criminal class, and acting in concert with a man. There is that about the act of battering in the skulls of an elderly man and woman which suggests the male butcher, not the more subtle though equally malicious methods of the murderess. The police of Fall River and the law officers of the county were not so inexperienced as to ignore this, and they could only have taken the step they did under the pressure of strong evidence. There was no lack of other and powerful influences working against it.

Mr. Edwin Porter's book, "The Fall River Tragedy" is a comprehensive history of the case based upon intimate personal knowledge.[3] It has the advantages and disadvantages of having been compiled, apparently, from current newspaper accounts, the result of the author's work as police reporter of *The Fall River Globe.* In the opening chapter, he sums up the perplexity which beset all early investigators. They were absolutely at a loss to explain how, in broad daylight, it had been possible

[3] See Appendix.

for anybody to commit two murders and escape unseen, both by those in and outside the house. This difficulty was increased as the medical testimony made it apparent that from one to two hours had elapsed between the death of Mrs. Borden and that of her husband. Mr. Porter refers to the escape of the murderer in one apt sentence: "The author of that hideous slaughter had come and gone as gently as the south wind, but had fulfilled his mission as terrifically as a cyclone."

In the same chapter he describes the extraordinary series of chances that favored the murderer. I quote the passage:

> To those who stop to contemplate the circumstances surrounding the double murder, it was marvelous to reflect how fortune had favored the assassin. Not once in a million times would fate have paved such a way for him. He had to deal with a family of six persons in an unpretentious two-and-a-half story house, the rooms of which were all connected and in which it would have been a difficult matter to stifle sound. He must catch Mr. Borden alone and either asleep, or off his guard, and kill him with one fell blow. The faintest outcry would have sounded an alarm. He must also encounter Mrs. Borden alone and fell her, a heavy woman, noiselessly. To do this he must either make his way from the sitting room on the ground floor to the spare bed room above the parlor and avoid five persons in the passage, or he must conceal himself in one of the rooms upstairs and make the

descent under the same conditions. The murdered woman must not lisp a syllable at the first attack, and her fall must not attract attention. He must then conceal the dripping implement of death and depart in broad daylight by a much frequented street. In order to accomplish this he must take a time, when Miss Emma L. Borden, the older daughter of the murdered man, was on a visit to relatives out of the city; Miss Lizzie A. Borden, the other daughter, must be in the barn and remain there twenty minutes. A less time than that would not suffice. Bridget Sullivan, the servant, must be in the attic asleep on her own bed. Her presence in the pantry or kitchen or any room on the first or second floors would have frustrated the fiend's designs, unless he also killed her so that she would die without a murmur. In making his escape there must be no blood stains upon his clothing; for such tell-tale marks might have betrayed him. And so, if the assailant of the aged couple was not familiar with the premises, his luck favored him exactly as described. He made no false move. He could not have proceeded more swiftly nor surely had he lived in the modest edifice for years. At the most he had just twenty minutes in which to complete his work. He must go into the house after Miss Lizzie entered the barn and he must disappear before she returned. More than that, the sixth member of the family, John V. Morse, must vanish from the house while the work was being done. He could not have been counted on by any criminal, however shrewd, who had planned the tragedy ahead. Mr. Morse came and went at the Borden homestead. He was not engaged in business in Fall River and there were no stated times when the wretch who did the slaughtering could depend upon his absence. Mr. Morse must not loiter about the house or yard after breakfast as was his custom; he must take a car to some other part of the city and he must not return until his host and hostess have been stretched lifeless. The slightest hitch in these conditions and the murderer would have been balked or detected red handed upon the spot. Had Miss Emma remained at home she would have been a stumbling block; had Miss Lizzie left the stable [barn] a few moments earlier she would have seen the murderer as he ran out the side door; had Bridget Sullivan shortened her nap and descended the stairs she would have heard her mistress drop, as the axe fell on her head; had Mr. Morse cut short his visit to friends by as much as ten minutes the butcher would have dashed into his arms as he ran out at the front gate; had Mr. Borden returned earlier from his morning visit to the post office he would have caught the assassin murdering his aged wife, or had he uttered a scream at the time he himself was cut down, at least two persons would have rushed to his assistance.

It was a wonderful chain of circumstances which conspired to clear the way for the murderer; so wonderful that its links baffled men's understanding.

There was still another and greater difficulty for this singularly astute and favored murderer to overcome. It is not clearly mentioned by Mr. Porter, for the reason, it may be, that his first chapter was written early in the history of the case and never revised in the light of subsequent knowledge. It was established that Mrs. Borden had been killed not less than an hour and possibly two hours before her husband. The autopsies proved this. Therefore it was necessary, assuming the murderer to have come from outside the house, for him to have killed Mrs. Borden at about half-past nine, without attracting the attention of Miss Lizzie Borden or of Bridget Sullivan; to have remained concealed in the house until eleven, still eluding them, and then to have accomplished his purpose with Mr. Borden, and to have left the house unseen. Even for those who advanced a different theory as to the identity of the murderer, that is, for persons who agreed with the contention of the Commonwealth, there were still unexplained difficulties,—especially as to the time of Mr. Morse's return and of Bridget's retirement upstairs. Who could have predicted when these would take place?

For those who like to exhaust every possibility, there is, of course, the wild hypothesis of a first and second murderer: one who killed Mrs. Borden and then fled, and one who tracked down and slew Mr. Borden in the same fashion, and with the same or similar weapon. Difficult, even absurd, as this theory is, it is no more impossible of belief than some of the notions which were entertained. Folk were almost ready to suggest a visitation of Providence, or other supernatural act of vengeance, although why the Heavenly powers should set upon this harmless pair was unexplained. Nor was the method exactly celestial.

The investigation went on during that hot afternoon, and before midnight the police had some astounding information. Dr. Bowen had related the story of the illness, and the suspected poisoning,—as Miss Borden had also done to Miss Russell and to Mrs. Churchill. Two officers went to various pharmacies to learn if anybody had been purchasing poison, and at D. R. Smith's on South Main Street, the clerk, Eli Bence, said that an attempt had been made to buy prussic-acid. This had happened on Wednesday, the day before the murders. A lady had come in the morning and asked for this deadly drug for the purpose of killing moths in a seal-skin coat. Mr. Bence had refused to sell it, except on a doctor's prescription, and she went away disappointed. He identified this lady as Miss Lizzie Borden, and, being taken to her house to see her, (although it is said that he knew her perfectly well by sight) persisted in the identification. In this he was supported by another clerk in the pharmacy, Frederick E. Hart, and by a third man who was also present, one Frank H. Kilroy. On the next day, August 5, *The Fall River Globe* printed a full account of it, under the headings: "What did Lizzie Want of Poison? She is Identified by a Drug Clerk as Having Visited his Store Recently." Newspapers elsewhere failed to accept the information, or else gave it slight attention. I have been told by one who knew him that Bence was a careful man, who was quite aware of the serious import of his statement. The final disposition of the matter, as legal evidence, will appear in an account of the trial.

The note, which, according to Miss Borden, had been received by her step-mother, remained elusive. Who had sent it? Who brought it? Under what circumstances was it received, and what action was taken? Did she really go out? Miss Borden thought she heard her come in. If she did go out, it is inconceivable that she went in the cotton dress in which she was doing house-work, and so it must have required agility to get back into that dress, for she wore it when death overtook her. A New York paper, *Once a Week*, offered $500 for the discovery of the writer of the note, and *The Fall River News* begged its readers in the name of justice, to find this writer. But the reward was unclaimed, and the appeal unanswered. Finally, Miss Borden told Dr. Dolan that she believed the note must have been burned up in the kitchen stove. Nobody suggested that the person who sent it and the messenger who brought it had been carried away by giant eagles. But the land knew them no more.

Within a single day the attention of the newspaper readers of the country was directed toward the Misses Borden. Miss Emma, the elder, had returned from Fairhaven in the evening of the day of the murder. Information about her was of a rather negative quality; she was reputed to be less active in church work than her sister, and to have traveled less. As to the younger, it never appeared that her parents had called her by the glorious name of Elizabeth; her legal style was that less pleasing diminutive, for which the best that can be said is that it did not offend the delicate ear of Miss Jane Austen, since she allowed the heroine of "Pride and Prejudice" so to be addressed by her family. In our time, the Ford automobile has been called, in derision, a Lizzie, and it is said that Miss Mary Pickford uses this name as a sort of generic term to describe her spectators. It can hardly be given in compliment. But in the years '92 and '93 there was only one "Lizzie" for the people of the United States, and it was that Fall River lady of medium figure and dark complexion who was presently to be confronted with the gravest of accusations. It is almost invariably noticed that a charge of murder, or of any serious crime, acts automatically to rob a person of all right to polite address; the public promptly makes free with the first name, especially if it is a woman. There is some strange rule about this, exactly as with the custom by which a sedate middle-aged man, when he puts on military uniform, in time of war, instantly becomes a "boy."

Miss Lizzie Borden was a native of Fall River, and had been graduated from the high school. Some of her classmates described her as "rather eccentric," which, of itself, means exactly nothing. There is no human being who would not be described as "eccentric," by one or another of his or her acquaintances. She had traveled in Europe, with other ladies, in 1890. Perhaps the outstanding fact about her was her membership in the Central Congregational Church, in various charitable societies such as the Fruit and Flower Mission, and in the Woman's Christian Temperance Union. At her Church Mission she taught a class of young people. Her association with these religious bodies was no meaningless fact when clouds began to gather over her life, for her cause was warmly supported by them. The Rev. Mr. Buck and the Rev. Mr. Jubb, her pastors, became her pillars of support, and although after a time, through constant repetition of their names, some of the less devout were tempted to look upon them as the Box and Cox of the Borden cause, it could have been no small consolation and of no little value to her, when she appeared at public hearings, to enter the room on some occasions "leaning on the arm" of the Rev. Mr. Buck, and at other times escorted in similar fashion by the Rev. Mr. Jubb.

The frank comments upon the case which appeared within the first few days may be typified by an interview given out on August 5th by Mr. Hiram Harrington. He was the husband of Mr. Borden's only sister, and is not to be confused with the officer, Philip Harrington. His remarks are given at length by Mr. Porter. A few passages may be quoted:

> Mr. Borden was an exceedingly hard man concerning money matters, determined and stubborn . . . As the motive for the crime it was money, unquestionably money. If Mr. Borden died he would have left something over $500,000, and in my opinion that estate furnishes the only motive, and a sufficient one for the double murder. Last evening I had a long interview with Miss Lizzie, who has refused to see anyone else. . . . She was very composed, showed no signs of any emotion, nor were there any traces of grief upon her coun-

> tenance. That did not surprise me, as she is not naturally emotional.

Then followed a description, quoted by Mr. Harrington, of Miss Borden's reception of her father when he returned on Thursday morning, her solicitous inquiries for his health, the assistance which she gave him in removing his coat, helping him to the sofa, and her offers to cover him with an afghan, and to lower the shades at the windows, so that he could have a "nice nap."

> On leaving the house, she says she went directly to the barn to obtain some lead. She informed me that it was her intention to go to Marion on a vacation, and she wanted the lead in the barn loft to make some sinkers. She was a very enthusiastic angler. I went over the ground several times and she repeated the same story.

Miss Borden, when questioned as to a possible explanation of the crime, told Mr. Harrington the story of the burglary in the house a year earlier, and of "strange men" recently seen by her around the house. She had been frightened enough to tell her parents about them, and to write to her sister at Fairhaven.

On the subject of the domestic and business affairs of the Borden family, Mr. Harrington said:

> Yes, there were family dissensions although it has been always kept very quiet. For nearly ten years there have been constant disputes between the daughters and their father and stepmother. It arose, of course, with regard to the stepmother.

Mr. Borden gave her some bank stock, and the girls thought they ought to be treated as evenly as the mother. I guess Mr. Borden did try to do it, for he deeded to the daughters, Emma L. and Lizzie A., the homestead on Ferry Street, an estate of 120 rods of land, with a house and barn, all valued at $3,000. This was in 1887. The trouble about money matters did not diminish, nor the acerbity of the family ruptures lessen, and Mr. Borden gave each girl ten shares in the Crystal Spring Bleachery Company, which he paid $100 a share for. They sold them soon after for less than $40 a share. He also gave them some bank stock at various times, allowing them of course, the entire income from them. In addition to this he gave them a weekly stipend, amounting to $200 a year. In spite of all this the dispute about their not being allowed enough went on with equal bitterness. Lizzie did most of the demonstrative contention, as Emma is very quiet and unassuming, and would feel deeply any disparaging or angry word from her father. Lizzie on the contrary, was haughty and domineering with the stubborn will of her father and bound to contest for her rights. There were many animated interviews between father and daughter on this point. Lizzie is of a repellent disposition, and after an unsuccessful passage with her father, would become sulky and refuse to speak to him for days at a time. She moved in the best society in Fall River, was a member of the Congregational Church, and is a brilliant con-

> versationalist. She thought she ought to entertain as others did, and felt that with her father's wealth she was expected to hold her end up with others of her set. Her father's constant refusal to allow her to entertain lavishly angered her. I have heard many bitter things she has said of her father, and know that she was deeply resentful of her father's maintained stand in this matter. This house on Ferry street was an old one, and was in constant need of repairs. There were two tenants paying $16.50 and $14 a month, but with taxes and repairs there was very little income from the property. It was a great deal of trouble for the girls to keep the house in repair, and a month or two ago they got disgusted and deeded the house back to their father. I am positive that Emma knows nothing of the murder.

The faction which held strong views about the stupidity of the Fall River police, and their brutal persecution of an innocent and bereaved woman, often said that the officers neglected all opportunities to catch the real murderer. The police formed a "theory," said their critics, and having done so, tried by all means—some of them unusually foul—to entangle their victim in it. In the opinion of the man in the street, who is supposed to be a devotee of "good, plain common-sense," it is, of course, a destructive thing to say of another man that he has a "theory." We know what Private Mulvaney thought of his lieutenant's fondness for theorizing.[4] Nobody should ever have any theories at all: but just plunge ahead. As a matter of truth, the police of Fall River spent weary hours and days in running down every report, rumor, and suspicion.

The usual crop of "strange," "wild" and "crazy" men, of tramps and vagrants, of "foreigners," and other guilty-looking persons was more prolific than ever. There was a suspected Portuguese, who was called a Portuguese because he was a Swede; and there were miscreants who turned up in lonely places, days and weeks after the murders, still brandishing axes or hatchets dripping with gore,—just as the Russian soldiers in England in August, 1914, still had—on their boots—the snow of their native land. Pale young men had been seen on Second Street. There was a camp of wandering horse-traders in Westport, and with them, it was alleged, Mr. John Vinnicum Morse had been darkly dealing. There was a disgruntled owner of property, across the river, whose business relations with Mr. Borden might have roused him to dreadful vengeance against all who bore the hated name. One Dr. Handy, who was on Second Street about an hour before the murders, had seen a very peculiar looking man, who attracted the doctor's most particular attention. This man was discussed, in column after column of newspaper space, as "Dr. Handy's Wild Eyed Man." Some participants in the discussion held that the Wild Eyed Man was better, but

[4] An allusion, by the way, which reminds me that there was something about the equipment of Mulvaney and the other captors of Lungtungpen which recalls a theory advanced in the Borden case.

still cryptically, known as "Mike the Soldier." Mike was run down and found free from all criminous taint, excepting that he was near Second Street about ten o'clock that morning, that he was pale, as a result of a spree, and that he wore an odd and noticeable pair of trousers. It appeared that he followed the weaver's trade, when he was not going from one bar-room to the next, and by talking with his fellow-weavers, and various saloon-keepers, it was easy to learn all that he had been doing, and to find that it was unimportant. But the Wild Eyed Man lingered, off-stage.

A boy had seen a man jump over the back fence of the Borden house. A Frenchman had helped the same man escape toward New Bedford, but how he knew it was the same man, in what way he helped him, and what he was escaping from, do not appear. Two officers found somebody like him in the person of the chief of the gypsy horse-dealers' camp. He had the satisfactory name of Bearsley S. Cooper, but he also had an alibi, which prevented anybody from visiting upon him the punishment which mankind always longs to inflict upon a horse-dealer. The terror of the murders had spread throughout New England, and men seen getting on railroad trains, or getting off them, with dust on their shoes, or spots on their clothes, were asked who they were, and what they had been doing. A Bostonian was frightened half to death by detention and questioning. On Monday another bloody hatchet was discovered on a farm in South Somerset; it was the property of somebody called Sylvia, and the police rushed out there, with the first words of the famous song trembling upon their lips. But the blood was the blood of a chicken, and old Mr. Sylvia was left undisturbed.

Petty offences hover close to great crimes, as the sucker follows the shark. When at some fête, during the French Revolution, two men were discovered lurking under a platform built for the spectators, they were charged with designs against the Republic, and promptly lynched by the mob. They went to their deaths, however, with the somewhat humiliating but probably truthful confession that gunpowder plots were far from their minds; they had gone there merely to gaze upwards at the sturdy legs of citizenesses. One man seen by a neighbor on the back fence of the Borden yard, was caught, and forced blushingly to admit that he had been attracted, as Mr. Morse had been, by the pears. But his interest was, of course, illicit, and hence his confusion. The police investigated every plausible rumor, and in order to deal according to precept with unturned stones, spent much good effort in many searches which were hopeless from the start. Their work at first was undoubtedly open to criticism, although metropolitan police often do no better with perplexing crimes. They finally arrived at a conclusion, and its results will appear in the account of the four legal investigations which followed.

Something should be said now about Bridget Sullivan, since she was in the house, or within a few feet of it, when each murder was committed. It has often been asked why she was not suspected. The answer is simple: she bore a good character, she had no motive to such crimes, and she was exonerated by the person who was still nearer to the scenes of the murders, Miss Lizzie

Borden herself. Vague suggestions of complicity, or guilty knowledge, arose against her, but evidently were not shared by the officers of the law. Bridget was an agitated and badly scared woman for a few days, and at last had to undergo a long cross-examination by one of the most skilful advocates in the State. It is said that she returned to her native land some years—not very long—after the trial, and there, an elderly woman, she may still abide, in the intermittent calm of the Irish Free State.

Of all the rumors as to murderers from the outside, only one had the charm of romance. Somebody attempted to inject a maritime flavor into the mystery, by recalling the trial, in 1876, of the mutineers on the schooner *Jefferson Borden.* It was suggested that Mr. Borden had an interest in this vessel, and that the guilty mutineers, imbued with the combined spirits of Clark Russell and Conan Doyle, had nursed their vengeful feelings for sixteen years, only to strike at last in this telling fashion. Unluckily for the story, it was discovered that two of the accused had been acquitted on their trial, one had served his term and now lived, crippled, in St. Paul; while the two ring-leaders were safe in the State Prison at Thomaston, Maine. Mr. Borden moreover, had no connection with the schooner.

On the day after the murders, this notice was sent to and duly appeared in the newspapers:

> "Five thousand dollars reward. The above reward will be paid to any one who may secure the arrest and conviction of the person or persons, who occa-

sioned the death of Andrew J. Borden and his wife.
Signed,

Emma L. Borden and Lizzie A. Borden."

The funeral services were held on Saturday, August 6. From three to four thousand people surrounded the house, and a passage was kept clear by twenty police officers. Other crowds of people lined the street as the hearses and the carriages with mourners proceeded to the cemetery. The coffins were not buried, but placed in a receiving tomb.

In the evening of that day, the Mayor of Fall River, Dr. John W. Coughlin, with City Marshal Hilliard, went to the Borden house. The number of people standing on the sidewalks or in the street itself was still so great that the mayor's carriage was driven with difficulty. Policemen were called and ordered to send the people away. The Mayor and the Marshal then went into the house to confer with the Misses Borden and Mr. Morse. Dr. Coughlin said:

"I have a request to make of the family, and that is that you remain in the house for a few days. I believe it would be better if you do so."

Miss Lizzie raised the question:

"Why, is there anybody in this house suspected?"

The Mayor answered: "Well, perhaps Mr. Morse can answer that question better than I, as his experience last night, perhaps, would justify him in the inference that somebody in the house is suspected."

Miss Lizzie persisted: "I want to know the truth."

And she repeated this remark. Then the Mayor said:

"Well, Miss Borden, I regret to answer, but I must answer yes; you are suspected."

She replied: "I am ready to go now."

Her sister said: "We have tried to keep it from her as long as we could."

Dr. Coughlin told the family that if they were disturbed in any way, or annoyed by the crowds in the street, they should either notify the officer in the yard, or send word to him—the Mayor—who would see that the police department gave them protection. Miss Emma Borden then remarked: "We want to do everything we can in this matter." And the two officials departed.

On the following Tuesday an investigation began, when Bridget Sullivan was examined by the District Attorney, Mr. Hosea M. Knowlton, assisted by the City Marshal, the Mayor, and the Medical Examiner. This investigation, on the same day, took the form of an inquest, before Judge Josiah C. Blaisdell of the Second District Court. A summons to attend was served upon Miss Lizzie Borden. Her family attorney, Mr. Andrew J. Jennings, appeared and made an appeal to the Court for permission to be present, "in the interests of the witnesses." The Justice heard his argument, but denied admission. The inquest continued its sessions in secret, until Thursday, while Fall River waited in suppressed excitement and impatience, reading newspaper bulletins, and learning nothing. The case was of such importance as to attract to the city the Attorney General of Massachusetts, Mr. Albert E. Pillsbury, who was in consultation with Mr. Knowlton and other officers. In addition to Miss Lizzie Borden, Dr. Bowen, Mrs. Churchill, Mr. Hiram Harrington, Mr. John Vinnicum Morse, and Miss Emma Borden were examined. Another witness, who was followed about in Fall River, and unsuccessfully questioned by the newspaper reporters was Professor Wood of the Harvard Medical School. On the third and last day of the inquest there appeared Eli Bence and the two other witnesses who were supposed to offer testimony as to the attempt to buy poison. On that same day autopsies were held, at the cemetery, upon the two bodies. Chiefly, they disclosed ten incised wounds on the head and face of Mr. Borden; and on the body of his wife, one wound in the back, just below the neck, and no less than eighteen incised and crushing wounds on the head.

The inquest ended late Thursday afternoon, one week after the murders. A short consultation was held and at the end of it, Mr. Jennings was called, and Miss Lizzie Borden arrested for the murder of her father. No mention of Mrs. Borden was made in the warrant. The prisoner was detained at the police station under charge of the matron, but she was not confined in the cell-room. Mr. Porter writes: "No other prisoner arrested in Bristol County had been accorded the delicate and patient consideration which Marshal Hilliard bestowed upon Miss Lizzie Borden."

She was arraigned in the District Court, before Judge Blaisdell next morning. She entered the room "on the arm of the Rev. Mr. Buck," and is described as wearing a dark blue suit, and a black hat with red flowers. She was "not crying, but her features were far from firm.

She has a face and chin betokening strength of character, and on this occasion the sensitiveness of the lips especially betrayed itself. She was constantly moving her lips as she sat in the court-room in a way to show that she was not altogether unemotional."

To the warrant, she pleaded not guilty. Mr. Jennings protested against the proceedings as "extraordinary," in that the Judge had presided at the inquest and was now sitting to hear the case against her. This he called sitting in a double capacity and not ensuring his client an unprejudiced hearing. The District Attorney replied that the statutes required Judge Blaisdell to hold the inquest, which was in itself an action against no one, but an attempt to ascertain facts. The same procedure had been followed more than twenty times to his knowledge in cases which had not excited so much attention. The inquest was still proceeding, and the evidence before it had no bearing upon this hearing. The Judge was equally required by statute to hear this case. The Court over-ruled Mr. Jennings's motion, and the point does not seem to have been raised again. The lawyers agreed upon August 22 for the preliminary hearing, and Miss Borden was taken by train to the jail at Taunton. At railway stations, and other places, crowds gathered to look at her.

On the date appointed Miss Borden was brought back to Fall River, but a postponement was made, until August 25. She remained in charge of the police matron, and was not taken back to Taunton. Finally, the hearings began. Crowds were present, inside and out of the court-room, and it is said that forty newspapers were represented by reporters. The prisoner entered the court, leaning upon the practised arm of the Rev. Mr. Buck. There began a preliminary trial which lasted for six days. Few such extensive investigations, prior to the presentation of a criminal case to the Grand Jury, could ever have been held in the State. Mr. Melvin O. Adams of Boston was now associated with Mr. Jennings in the defence. The witnesses included the Medical Examiner, Dr. Dolan; Thomas Kieran, an engineer, who gave technical details about measurements of the Borden house; officers of the banks which Mr. Borden had visited the day he was killed; John Vinnicum Morse; Bridget Sullivan; Mrs. Churchill; Miss Alice Russell, who testified only as to events on the day of the murder; Eli Bence and the other men from the pharmacy,—whose appearance, says Mr. Porter, "in the judgment of many of the spectators . . . produced evidence of uneasiness on the part of Lizzie Borden," and some officers of the police.

On the fifth day of the hearing, Professor Wood's evidence was given. It was to the effect that his tests and analyses of the two stomachs showed that digestion was much further advanced with Mr. Borden than with his wife. There was about two and a half hours' difference.[5] No trace of prussic acid was found in either stomach; tests were not made for any other poison, but there was no evidence of irritation. He had made examinations for blood stains on a hatchet and two axes, found in the Borden house, and on a dress waist, two skirts, and shoes and stockings belonging to the prisoner. Except for a

[5] Either a mistake in the report, or an opinion altered later. Professor Wood's final estimate was about an hour and a half.

minute spot on one of the skirts, he found no blood upon any of these. This testimony was received with great relief and joy by the friends of Miss Borden; quite naturally and correctly they looked upon it as a strong point in her favor.

After some more police evidence, the District Attorney read the short-hand report of the testimony of Miss Lizzie Borden given at the inquest. This is an exceedingly interesting and important series of questions and answers. Miss Borden, as we have seen, talked to friends and neighbors and to the police, on the day of the murders. Afterwards, except for the inquest statement, she never opened her mouth. She acted upon what proved to be the best of legal advice, and at her final trial, availed herself of her right not to go upon the witness stand. The report of the proceedings at the inquest is not available today; I am not sure that it is in existence. Miss Borden's testimony at the inquest introduced at the preliminary trial, as part of the case of the Commonwealth, is significant not only for itself but for the point raised when it was offered as evidence at the trial before the Superior Court. It is to be found today only in the press reports of that date, and in Mr. Porter's book,—to which I am so much indebted for information about this period in the history of the case. I quote his version of it.

> My father and stepmother were married twenty-seven years ago. I have no idea how much my father was worth and have never heard him form an opinion. I know something about what real estate my father owned . . . "two farms in Swansea, the

homestead, some property on North Main street, Borden Block, some land further south and some he had recently purchased." "Did you ever deed him any property?" "He gave us some land, but my father bought it back. Had no other transaction with him. He paid in five thousand dollars cash for this property. Never knew my father made a will, but heard so from Uncle Morse." "Did you know of anybody that your father had trouble with?" "There was a man who came there some weeks before, but I do not know who he was. He came to the house one day, and I heard them talk about a store. My father told him he could not have a store. The man said: 'I thought with your liking for money you would let anybody in.' I heard my father order him out of the house. Think he lived out of town, because he said he could go back and talk with father." "Did your father and anybody else have bad feelings between them?" "Yes, Hiram C. Harrington. He married my father's only sister." "Nobody else?" "I have no reason to suppose that that man had seen my father before that day." "Did you ever have any trouble with your stepmother?" "No." "Within a year?" "No." "Within three years?" "No. About five years ago." "What was it about?" "About my stepmother's stepsister, Mrs. George Whitehead." "Was it a violent expression of feeling?" "It was simply a difference of opinion." "Were you always cordial with your stepmother?" "That depends upon one's idea of cordiality." "Was it cordial according to your ideas of cordiality?" "Yes." Continuing: "I did not regard her as my mother, though she came there when I was young. I decline to say whether my relations between her and myself were those of mother and daughter or not. I called her Mrs. Borden and sometimes mother. I stopped calling her mother after the affair regarding her sister-in-law." "Why did you leave off calling her mother?" "Because I wanted to." "Have you any other answer to give me?" "No, sir. I always went to my sister. She was older than I was. I don't know but that my father and stepmother were happily united. I never knew of any difficulty between them, and they seemed to be affectionate. The day they were killed I had on a blue dress. I changed it in the afternoon and put on a print dress. Mr. Morse came into our house whenever he wanted to. He has been here once since the river was frozen over. I don't know how often he came to spend the nights, because I had been away so much. I have not been away much during the year. He has been there very little during the past year. I have been away a great deal in the daytime during the last year. I don't think I have been away much at night, except once when I was in New Bedford. I was abroad in 1890. I first saw Morse Thursday noon. Wednesday evening I was with Miss Russell at 9 o'clock, and I don't know whether the family were in or not. I went direct to my room. I locked the front door when I came in. Was in my room Wednesday, not feeling well all day. Did not go down to supper. Went out that evening and came in and locked the front door. Came down about 9 next morning. Did not inquire about Mr. Morse that morning. Did not go to Marion at that time, because they could go sooner than I. I had taken the Secretaryship of the Christian Endeavor Society and had to remain over till the 10th. There had been nobody else around there that week but the man I have spoken of. I did not say that he came a week before, but that week. Mr. Morse slept in the spare room Wednesday night. It was my habit to close my room door when I was in it. That Wednesday afternoon they made such a noise that I closed the door. First saw my father Thursday morning down stairs reading the *Providence Journal*. Saw my mother with a dust cloth in her hand. Maggie was putting a cloth into a mop. Don't know whether I ate cookies and tea that morning. Know the coffee pot was on the stove. My father went down town after 9 o'clock. I did not finish the handkerchiefs because the irons were not right. I was in the kitchen reading when he returned. I am not sure that I was in the kitchen when my father returned. I stayed in my room long enough to sew a piece of lace on a garment. That was before he came back. I don't know where Maggie was. I think she let my father in, and that he rang the bell. I understood Maggie to say he said he had forgotten his key. I think I was up stairs when my father came in, and I think I was on the stairs when he entered.

don't know whether Maggie was washing windows or not when my father came in." At this point the District Attorney had called Miss Borden's attention to her conflicting statements regarding her position when her father came in, and her answer was: "You have asked me so many questions, I don't know what I have said." Later, she said she was reading in the kitchen and had gone into the other room for a copy of the *Providence Journal*. "I last saw my mother when I was down stairs. She was dusting the dining room. She said she had been up stairs and made the bed and was going up stairs to put on the pillow slips. She had some cotton cloth pillows up there, and she said she was going to work on them. If she had remained down stairs I should have seen her. She would have gone up the back way to go to her room. If she had gone to the kitchen I would have seen her. There is no reason to suppose I would not have seen her when she was down stairs or in her room, except when I went down stairs once for two or three minutes." "I ask you again what you suppose she was doing from the time you saw her till 11 o'clock?" "I don't know, unless she was making her bed." "She would have had to pass your room, and you would have seen her, wouldn't you?" "Yes, unless I was in my room or down cellar. I supposed she had gone away, because she told me she was going, and we talked about the dinner. Didn't hear her go out or come back. When I first came down stairs saw Maggie coming in, and my mother asked me how I was feeling. My father was still there, still reading. My mother used to go and do the marketing." "Now I call your attention to the fact you said twice yesterday that you first saw your father after he came in when you were standing on the stairs." "I did not. I was in the kitchen when he came in, or in one of the three rooms, the dining room, kitchen and sitting room. It would have been difficult for anybody to pass through these rooms unless they passed through while I was in the dining room." "A portion of the time the girl was out of doors, wasn't she?" "Yes." "So far as I know, I was alone in the house the larger part of the time while my father was away. I was eating a pear when my father came in. I had put a stick of wood into the fire to see if I could start it. I did no more ironing after my father came in. I then went in to tell him. I did not put away the ironing board. I don't know what time my father came in. When I went out to the barn I left him on the sofa. The last thing I said was to ask him if he wanted the window left that way. Then I went to the barn to get some lead for a sinker. I went upstairs in the barn. There was a bench there which contained some lead. I unhooked the screen door when I went out. I don't know when Bridget got through washing the windows inside. I knew she washed the windows outside. I knew she didn't wash the kitchen windows, but I don't know whether she washed the sitting room windows or not. I thought the flats would be hot by the time I got back. I had not fishing apparatus, but there was some at the farm. It is five years since I used the fish line. I don't think there was any sinker on my line. I don't think there were any fish lines suitable for use at the farm." "What! did you think you would find sinkers in the barn?" "My father once told me that there was some lead and nails in the barn." "How long do you think you occupied in looking for the sinkers?" "About fifteen or twenty minutes." "Did you do nothing besides look for sinkers in the twenty minutes?" "Yes, sir. I ate some pears." "Would it take you all that time to eat a few pears?" "I do not do things in a hurry." "Was Bridget not washing the dining room windows and the sitting room windows?" "I do not know. I did not see her." "Did you tell Bridget to wash the windows?" "No, sir." "Who did?" "My mother." "Did you see Bridget after your mother told her to wash the windows?" "Yes, sir." "What was she doing?" "She had got a long pole and was sticking it in a brush, and she had a pail of water." "About what time did you go out into the barn?" "About as near as I can recollect, 10 o'clock." "What did you go into the barn for?" "To find some sinkers." "How many pears did you eat in that twenty minutes?" "Three." "Is that all you did?" "No. I went over to the window and opened it." "Why did you that?" "Because it was too hot." "I suppose that it is the hottest place on the premises?" "Yes, sir." "Could you, while standing looking out of that window, see anybody enter the kitchen?"

"No, sir." "I thought you said you could see people from the barn?" "Not after you pass a jog in the barn. It obstructs the view of the back door." "What kind of lead were you looking for, for sinkers? Hard lead?" "No, sir; soft lead." "Did you expect to find the sinkers already made?" "Well, no. I thought I might find one with a hole through it." "Was the lead referred to tea lead or lead that comes in tea chests?" "I don't know." "When were you going fishing?" "Monday." "The next Monday after the fatal day?" "Yes, sir." "Had you lines all ready?" "No, sir." "Did you have a line?" "Yes, sir." "Where was your line?" "Down to the farm." "Do you know whether there were any sinkers on the line you left at the farm?" "I think there was none on the line." "Did you have any hooks?" "No, sir." "Then you were making all this preparation without either hook or line. Why did you go into the barn after sinkers?" Because I was going down town to buy some hooks and line, and thought it would save me from buying them." "Now, to the barn again. Do you not think I could go into the barn and do the same as you in a few minutes?" "I do not do things in a hurry." "Did you then think there were no sinkers at the barn?" "I thought there were no sinkers anywhere there. I had no idea of using my lines. I thought you understood that I wasn't going to use these lines at the farm, because they hadn't sinkers. I went upstairs to the kind of bench there. I had heard my father say there was lead there. Looked for lead in a box up there. There were nails and perhaps an old door knob. Did not find any lead as thin as tea lead in the box. Did not look anywhere except on the bench. I ate some pears up there. I have now told you everything that took place up in the barn. It was the hottest place in the premises. I suppose I ate my pears when I first went up there. I stood looking out of the window. I was feeling well enough to eat pears, but don't know how to answer the question if I was feeling better than I was in the morning, because I was feeling better that morning. I picked the pears up from the ground. I was not in the rear of the barn. I was in the front of it. Don't see how anybody could leave the house then without my seeing them. I pulled over boards to look for the lead. That took me some time. I returned from the barn and put my hat in the dining room. I found my father and called to Maggie. I found the fire gone out. I went to the barn because the irons were not hot enough and the fire had gone out. I made no efforts to find my mother at all. Sent Maggie for Dr. Bowen. Didn't see or find anything after the murders to tell me my mother had been sewing in the spare room that morning." "What did your mother say when you saw her?" "She told me she had had a note and was going out. She said she would get the dinner." The District Attorney continued to read: "My mother did not tell when she was coming back. I did not know Mr. Morse was coming to dinner. I don't know whether I was at tea Wednesday night or not. I had no apron on Thursday; that is, I don't think I had. I don't remember surely. I had no occasion to use the axe or hatchet. I knew there was an old axe down stairs and last time I saw it it was on the old chopping block. I don't know whether my father owned a hatchet or not. Assuming a hatchet was found in the cellar I don't know how it got there, and if there was blood on it I have no idea as to how it got there. My father killed some pigeons last May. When I found my father I did not think of Mrs. Borden, for I believed she was out. I remember asking Mrs. Churchill to look for my mother. I left the screen door closed when I left, and it was open when I came from the barn. I can give no idea of the time my father came home. I went right to the barn. I don't know whether he came to the sitting room at once or not. I don't remember his being in the sitting room or sitting down. I think I was in there when I asked him if there was any mail. I do not think he went upstairs. He had a letter in his hand. I did not help him to lie down and did not touch the sofa. He was taking medicine for some time. Mrs. Borden's father's house was for sale on Fourth street. My father bought Mrs. Borden's half sister's share and gave it to her. We thought what he did for her people he ought to do for his own and he then gave us grandfather's house. I always thought my stepmother induced him to purchase the interest. I don't know when the windows were last washed before that day. All day Tuesday I was at the table. I gave the officer the same skirt I wore that day, and if there was any blood on it I can give an explanation as to how it got there. If the blood came from the outside, I cannot say how it got there. I wore tie shoes that day and black stockings. I was under the pear trees four or five minutes. I came down the front stairs when I came down in the morning. The dress I wore that forenoon was a white and blue stripe of some sort. It is at home in the attic. I did not go to Smith's drug store to buy prussic acid. Did not go to the rooms where mother or father lay after the murder. Went through when I went up stairs that day." . . . "I now ask if you can furnish any other suspicion concerning any person who might have committed the crime?" "Yes; one night as I was coming home not long ago I saw the shadow of a man on the house at the east end. I thought it was a man because I could not see any skirts. I hurried in the front door. It was about 8:45 o'clock; not later than 9. I saw somebody run around the house last winter. The last time I saw anybody lately was since my sister went to Marion. I told Mr. Jennings, may have told Mr. Hanscom." "Who suggested the reward offered, you or your sister?" "I don't know. I may have."

Mr. Knowlton stopped reading, and said: "This is the case of the Commonwealth."

The defence called Dr. Bowen and Marshal Hilliard. On the sixth day of the trial, arguments of counsel were presented at a length hardly less than at a trial before a jury. At the conclusion of the speech of the prosecuting attorney, Judge Blaisdell said:

"The long examination is now concluded, and there remains for the magistrate to perform what he believes to be his duty. It would be a pleasure for him, and he would doubtless receive much sympathy if he could say, 'Lizzie, I judge you probably not guilty. You may go home.' But upon the character of the evidence presented through the witnesses who have been so closely and thoroughly examined, there is but one thing to be done. Suppose for a single moment a man was standing there. He was found close by that guest chamber, which, to Mrs. Borden, was a chamber of death. Suppose a man had been found in the vicinity of Mr. Borden; was the first to find the body, and the only account he could give of himself was the unreasonable one that he was out in the barn looking for sinkers; then he was out in the yard; then he was out for something else; would there be any question in the minds of men what should be done with such a man?"

There was a pause, and the old Judge's eyes filled with tears.

"So there is only one thing to do, painful as it may be—the judgment of the Court is that you are probably guilty, and you are ordered committed to await the action of the Superior Court."

If the tide seemed to set against Miss Borden, and if the preliminary skirmishes had given distress to those who had already acquitted her in their minds, it must not be supposed that her friends, including a number of highly respected and influential persons, were not gathering valiantly. The painful situation in which she found herself, her sex, and her religious associations, were summoning to her aid many people from all parts of the State,—persons who had hitherto been strangers to her. The points which had told against her were the seemingly impossible nature of the story about the visit to the barn or yard; the alleged attempt to buy poison; the lapse of time between the two murders, which appeared to shake the theory of an outside murderer; the failure to find the sender of the note to Mrs. Borden; and the fact that from the stairs which she descended when her father entered the house, the body of her step-mother could have been visible. But, on the other hand, the glaring improbability of such murders being committed by a woman; combined with the failure to find any definitely determined weapon; and above everything, the absence of blood from the clothing or person of the accused,—all these not only strengthened the faith of those who were sure of her innocence, but convinced the authorities that they were far from having a strong case.

Her defence, so far as concerns those in whose hands it was officially placed, was conducted with wisdom, dignity, and propriety.

Elsewhere, however, there was more than the usual amount of irresponsible agitation, gushing sentimentality, and abuse of officers of the government who were merely bent on the disagreeable task of carrying out their plain and imperative duties. The abuse was the more disgusting since much of it originated with persons of education and self-professed moral superiority. The lynching mob exists in America in two forms, equally discouraging to those who cling to their faith in democracy: the mob which hunts down and kills some wretch of a malefactor, or alleged malefactor; and the mob which rails against legal officers who are engaged in protecting the community against crime. Some newspaper writers and public personages, men and women, took up Miss Borden's cause with no other equipment than ignorance. Blatantly they abused the Judge, the District Attorney and the police. One editorial writer was outraged in his feelings because of the "harshness" of the words used in the warrant for arrest, as if a charge of murder should be conveyed in terms of delicate insinuation. To tell him that the form of complaint was a hundred and fifty years old would have availed nothing; so excited was he in behalf of the "unfortunate girl" that he would have suggested an agreeable form for this case. The Rev. Mr. Jubb said that the action of Judge Blaisdell in sitting on the bench, after presiding at the inquest, was "indecent, outrageous and not to be tolerated in any civilized community." To him it was mildly remarked that the statute under which the Judge acted had been in use in America nearly two hundred years, and somewhat antedated his own personal knowledge of this country, since he had come hither from England within about one year.

Associations like the Woman's Auxiliary of the Y.M.C.A. took up Miss Borden's cause, sometimes with enthusiasm and knowledge; sometimes merely with enthusiasm. Prayers were invited from religious societies all over the country, the verdict was found in advance, and Heaven was to be implored or advised to assist the "unfortunate girl." There was an unpleasant flavor of sectarianism about much of this agitation; innocence must be assumed because of church membership. In contradistinction to this, however, I have seen proof that some of the more thoughtful of the lady's spiritual brethren, including clergymen in different parts of the State, had no sympathy with the attempts to interfere with law by the methods of the revival and the camp-meeting. As to the term which was applied to her, it is, of course, conventional to refer to anybody accused of a capital crime as "this girl" or "this boy" provided that she or he is still under sixty years of age. And for the other word, Mr. Porter said that throughout the whole proceeding, Miss Borden was called "unfortunate," but that nobody, good, bad, or indifferent, was ever heard to say that the murdered man and woman were "unfortunate."

Ten thousand tears are shed in America for persons accused of murder, and even for persons convicted of murder, to every word of regret spoken for the victims of the murders. And that, according to thoughtful investigators, is one of the reasons why America leads the world in its shameful record for the unlawful taking of human life,—although a few semi-civilized Oriental countries, and certain turbulent provinces of Italy, may be exceptions to this statement.

Advocates of suffrage for women came energetically to the defence of Miss Borden, almost as if her sex alone proved her innocence. One especially good result of the present status of women as voters, is a nearly complete abandonment on the part of their political leaders of the belief which was prevalent thirty or forty years ago: that all women accused of grave crimes should either be cleared in advance of trial, or if convicted, should not be liable for punishment. Their present attitude is a far more reasonable acceptance of women's duties and responsibilities to the State, as no more and no less than those of men. But in 1892, Mrs. Mary A. Livermore, an estimable lady of very vigorous character, Mrs. Susan Fessenden, president of the Woman's Christian Temperance Union, and Miss Lucy Stone, all distinguished in the struggle for what were then termed "Woman's Rights," came to the aid and comfort of Miss Borden. They did it so ecstatically as to leave doubt whether they were acting from logic or from emotion.

Miss Borden's name means little today to those who do not remember the year of her trial. Perhaps the younger folk in Scotland have never heard of Madeleine Smith, although their fathers and grandfathers followed her adventures with palpitating interest. Soon, perhaps, the name of Mrs. Maybrick will have completely faded from memory in England and America. One may search old books on criminology and summon one's own recollections, in vain, to recall the name of any American woman, resting under the capital charge, which was so widely known as that of Miss Borden. Perhaps the equally unfortunate Miss Nan Patterson is the only one for comparison, although far in the past they heard of Mrs. Cunningham, more recently arose the grim figure of Mrs. Rogers of Vermont, and the adventurous Clara Phillips of California. No *Ballade des Dames du Temps Jadis* celebrates these names; they, too, are gone with the snows of yester-year. But once, upon railroad trains, in clubs, at tea-parties, and around every breakfast table could be heard conversations about "Lizzie." A voice would arise from a group of talkers, anywhere between the two oceans: "I tell you, she never did it in the world! It's impossible. I *know* she never did it!" And nobody had to ask what was being discussed.

An account of the case would be incomplete if it did not record the fact that, however unjustly, the event was celebrated in rhyme, in one of those jingles which are never forgotten. Who invented it, nobody knows, but everyone heard it:

Lizzie Borden took an axe
And gave her Mother forty whacks;
When she saw what she had done,—
She gave her Father forty-one!

This has been communicated to me, in one way or another, at least half a dozen times, while I have been writing this article, by persons to whom it was the most vivid recollection of the Fall River murders,—surpassing even the mutton-soup. Miss Carolyn Wells told me that once, when she was repeating some limericks and nonsense rhymes to President Roosevelt, on the veranda at Sagamore Hill, he recited this, and said that of all the doggerel verse he had ever heard, it had remained most persistently in his mind.

Similar folk-rhymes have been associated with two

notorious crimes in Great Britain: one which delighted Sir Walter Scott:

> They cut his throat from ear to ear
>   His brains they battered in;
> His name was Mr. William Weare,
>   He dwelt in Lyon's Inn,

and that even grimmer quatrain which sums up the popular notion—as these things do—of the West Port murders in Edinburgh:

> Up the close and doun the stair,
> But and ben wi' Burke and Hare,
> Burke's the butcher, Hare's the thief,
> Knox the boy that buys the beef.

In America there is hardly a notorious murder which does not evoke one or two jokes or epigrams, sometimes witty, sometimes ribald, but only one other beside the Fall River murder, has, to my knowledge, brought forth any rhyme. In the early '90's, one Isaac Sawtell, living in New Hampshire, planned to do away with his brother, Hiram. He noted with approval that the neighboring State of Maine, more considerate toward gentlemen of his disposition than his own New Hampshire, had abolished the death penalty. So he took his brother out for a drive one evening, crossed, as he thought, into Maine, and killed him. But his topographical sense was at fault; the deed had really been done in New Hampshire after all, and that State, with its more ancient and barbarous laws, dealt with him in the end,—a fact which should have grieved every humanitarian. The incident was described in a couplet by some Cockney rhymster:

**Two brothers in our town did dwell,**
**Hiram sought Heaven, but Isaac Sawtell.**

Miss Borden went back to the jail in Taunton, to await the action of the Grand Jury. It was with her as with the Napoleonic prisoners in "Peter Ibbetson": she could not have found her durance very vile. I have been credibly informed that she was seen on the streets of Taunton, from time to time, having been taken out for walks. Whether this privilege was accorded because of the advance decision of her innocence, or because she was joint-heiress to a considerable estate, there is no information.

In October occurred a thoroughly discreditable incident. At first it seemed to be a heavy blow at Miss Borden's interests, but its effect was almost instantly reversed, and in the end probably worked in her favor. A newspaper reporter with the felicitous name of Henry G. Trickey, and a detective named Edwin D. McHenry were concerned in the production of a long newspaper article with which somebody hoodwinked *The Boston Globe.* Trickey and his friends blamed McHenry for it, while McHenry and his friends blamed Trickey. Definitely it can be said that Trickey was indicted by the Grand Jury for his part in the affair, that he left the country and did not live to return, nor to meet the accusation.

A newspaper seldom publishes such an article. It began on the front page of the *Globe*, on October 10, and filled nearly two and a half of its pages. In all these columns, which purported to set forth testimony in possession of the Government, truth rarely entered. Had one-quarter of it been fact, it would have convicted the prisoner. The *prima facie* case for the prosecution must have seemed, to outsiders, to be strong indeed, or this could not have appeared. The names of the newly discovered witnesses were plausible, although they were nearly all imaginary. A man called John H. Murphy, while passing the house, had seen Miss Borden in Mrs. Borden's room. Another mythical person, "Mrs. Gustave F. Ronald," had passed the house at 9.40, had heard a terrible cry, and had seen a woman whose head was covered with a rubber cap, or hood. (It was a favorite theory, at this time, that the mysterious assassin had worn some outside covering for the hair to avoid being spattered with blood. Some newspapers and their readers found a still greater thrill in the notion that the assailant of the Bordens had dispensed with clothing altogether during the commission of the deed.) A certain "Peter Mahany" had witnessed all that "Mrs. Ronald" had seen, and, in addition, had recognized the hooded woman as the prisoner. The street opposite must have thronged with witnesses! Mr. and Mrs. Frederick Chace, calling at the house on Wednesday evening, had overheard a quarrel between Mr. Borden and his younger daughter,—about a man, a lover. This seemed at last to bring into the case the "love interest," for which many newspaper reporters had almost pined away and died. Bridget Sullivan (an actual person at last) was to tell of a quarrel which happened the same evening. The police matron was to amplify an adverse bit of testimony—already in evidence—and to say that she had heard Miss Borden tell John Vinnicum Morse to "get those things out of the way in my room, and then they can do their worst."

On the following day the *Globe* made a partial retraction. "It [the story] has been proven wrong in some particulars." Mr. McHenry, the *Globe* said, had furnished the story, and admits that the names and addresses of witnesses were purposely false. The other Boston papers were quoted as denying the truth of the yarn. One part which was entirely withdrawn—to the sorrow of all good reporters—was the "love interest." Finally, on October 12, the *Globe*, in a boxed article on the front page, made a full retraction. It had been "grievously misled," suffered an "imposition," "unparalleled . . . cunningly contrived" but "based on facts." It expressed its "heartfelt apology" for the "inhuman reflection" on Miss Borden's honor, and included in the apology, Mr. John Vinnicum Morse.

Mr. Trickey soon left Boston, and in November he was killed by a railroad train in Canada. It may be imagined that more than one of Miss Borden's rural neighbors and sympathizers solemnly remarked: "It was a *jedgment* on him!" The final result of this wretched affair may well have been to add to the number of those who distrust the newspapers, and to persuade them that if this damaging story had been acknowledged as false, everything which seemed to tell against the prisoner might equally be false.

The Grand Jury of Bristol met in November and listened to the evidence for a week. An unusual course was followed in that the District Attorney, Mr. Knowlton, invited Miss Borden's counsel, Mr. Jennings, to be present and offer evidence for the defence. It is not customary for the Grand Jury to hear others beside the witnesses for the prosecution. The sitting was adjourned until December 1, when a curious thing happened. Miss Alice Russell re-appeared and gave testimony which had not been offered before. On December 2, the Grand Jury found three indictments against Miss Borden: one for the murder of her father, one for the murder of her stepmother, and one in which she was charged with both murders. Mr. Porter says that there were twenty-one jurymen present when the vote was taken; twenty voted "guilty," and one voted against that finding.

In the months which followed the preliminary trial, and especially in the autumn of 1892, the District Attorney made a careful study of the case, and pursued investigations in various directions. The members of the Grand Jury, after they completed their work, had desired to draw up a paper certifying to the impartial manner in which he had presented the case for the Government, but he advised them not to do so. The question of the prisoner's sanity had been raised, soon after the arrest, and inquiries were made into the family history, but with negative results. Miss Borden had more than once spoken of the burglary of the house, which had taken place a year before the murders, and as the police had been consulted at the time, they were asked for a report of the circumstances.

In the latter part of June, 1891, so it appeared, Mr. Borden had called upon City Marshal Hilliard, and asked that officer's help. A police captain was detailed to go with Mr. Borden to the house on Second Street, where they found Mrs. Borden, the Misses Borden, and Bridget Sullivan. In a small room on the second floor, Mr. Borden's desk had been broken open. Eighty dollars in "money" (bank-notes?), twenty-five or thirty in gold, a large number of street-car tickets, Mrs. Borden's watch with a chain, and some other small trinkets had been stolen. The family were at a loss to see how any one could get in and out unseen. Miss Lizzie Borden said: "The cellar door was open, and someone might have come in that way." The officer visited the houses in the neighborhood and exhausted all the resources of the average detective who is not the creation of a novelist: that is, he asked if anybody had seen a mysterious stranger entering the Borden house. One "clew" he did get: Miss Lizzie Borden presented him with "a 6 or 8 penny nail" which she had found in the keyhole of a bed-room door. Apparently nobody seemed to think that the robber, in leaving this behind him, had made an adequate return for his thefts. Three times within two weeks, said the officer, Mr. Borden remarked to him: "I am afraid the police will not be able to find the real thief." He was right, and the robbery, like the greater crime in that household, remains a mystery.

We usually read, during the investigation of a notorious crime, that the police, or the prosecuting officers, or the attorneys for the defence, or the Governor, are receiving hundreds or thousands of letters from cranks and others; suggestions, insinuations, accusations, and threats. As few of us are policemen, criminal lawyers, or Governors, we take this for granted and seldom expect to see such letters; perhaps we would rather not see them. It has been my privilege to read five or six large packets of communications received by the District Attorney during his investigation of these murders, and a more curious and varied collection could not be imagined. From all parts of the United States they came; written on all possible colors and shapes of paper, in every type of hand-writing, and every degree of sanity. Excitable, calm, puerile, nonsensical, pompous, intelligent (a few), preposterous, or insulting, they poured in by the dozen. A railroad conductor in the West asked Mr. Knowlton to lay aside his official duties, and embark upon genealogical research, which had no reference to the crime. An embattled Protestant from Vermont called upon him to clap Bridget Sullivan and her "confessor" into prison, and extort admissions from them,—apparently by torture. He ended: "beware of jesuits." A man in Albany gleefully admitted that he alone was guilty in this case (he had many a rival in his claim!), but that he was "moving about so fast" that the police could not hope to catch him. Spiritualists, clairvoyants, crystal-gazers, and other seers had discovered strange things under the flooring of the Borden house, or concealed in the stuffing of the "sopha." The Ouija board had been invoked, and had answered a long series of questions in its maddening fashion,—half devil and half child. Its control was much interested in "Lizzie's cat," that doubtful animal, which, so it was alleged, had been treated with such slight consideration by its mistress.

One bold blade, who signed "Voter," wrote an abusive post-card, to inform Mr. Knowlton that he deserved to be "kicked out" and that he would never again be District Attorney,—a sound prophecy, since he was soon promoted by the voters of the State to the office of Attorney General.

Many of the letters began with apologies, and assurances that the writers were acting solely in the interests of justice, but a lady from Brooklyn with a romantic name, an adherent to the most popular theory of all, closed by saying: "If the suggestions prove of any value, I shall expect to be suitably rewarded." The attorney was advised to hunt for the missing weapon in the piano, in the back of the kitchen stove, in the barn, the outhouses, and the well. The thought that the police might have looked in some of these places did not occur to the letter-writers. One man, who sent in some curious and rather acute messages, wrote that if the search continued unsuccessful, the house should be burned down in order to find the weapon, as nobody, in his opinion, would ever wish to live in it again. He cited the Burdell and Nathan houses in New York, in support of this theory, but he was mistaken, since the house is cheerfully occupied at the present time.

A band of letter-writers were convinced that the weapon had been, not a hatchet, but a flat-iron, and upon this contention they wrote pages. A serious correspondent from Danvers, Massachusetts, proposed that both men and women should be set to work battering the skulls of subjects in the dissecting-room, in order to prove experimentally the difference between blows inflicted by persons of opposite sexes. Two or three correspondents suggested that the Fall River murderer was probably

Such-a-One who murdered Somebody in 1884, or Another Man who killed Some-One-Else-Again in 1879,—the fancy being that there are only one or two murderers in the land, and that they go about from place to place, like traveling salesmen, or the public hangman in England. But by far the most popular theory was that held by the "water-proof" or "gossamer" school. The idea that the clothes of the assailant of the Bordens might have been protected from blood-stains by a water-proof, to be washed or destroyed, was widely entertained and plausibly argued.

Perhaps the most intelligent letter of all came from a lady, who also wrote to the Attorney General. Her suggestion was that there was something curious in the action of the discoverer of the body of the dead man, in remaining in that fatal house, where for all anybody could know, the murderer was still lurking. Another suggestion was that the absence of blood stains from clothing, might well prove too much, when that clothing was worn by the child of a murdered man, who was the first to discover the death. Both of these facts in the Borden case, by the way, offer a striking comparison to certain incidents in the Nathan murder, described later in this book. There was a similar situation there, but the results were quite different.

Six months elapsed between the indictment and the trial before the Superior Court, one of the almost invariable delays of our law, but one which provoked no complaint from the defence. The situation was unusual, and it is best indicated by a letter from the District Attorney to the Attorney General, written in the spring.

The Borden House in 1892
At the time of the murders

The Borden House
As it looks now

A capital case in Massachusetts is frequently prosecuted for the State by the Attorney General, but Mr. Pillsbury was not in good health. Mr. Knowlton, in this letter of April 24, 1893, said, among other things:

"Personally I would like very much to get rid of the trial of the case, and fear that my own feelings in that direction may have influenced my better judgment. I feel this all the more upon your not unexpected announcement that the burden of the trial will come upon me.

"I confess, however, I cannot see my way clear to any disposition of the case other than a trial. Should it result in disagreement of the jury there would be no difficulty then in disposing of the case by admitting the defendant to bail: but a verdict either way would render such a course unnecessary.

"The case has proceeded so far and an indictment has been found by the grand inquest of the county that it does not seem to me that we ought to take the responsibility of discharging her without trial, even though there is every reasonable expectation of a verdict of not guilty. I am unable to concur fully in your views as to the probable result. I think it may well be that the jury might disagree upon the case. But even in my most sanguine moments I have scarcely expected a verdict of guilty.

"The situation is this: nothing has developed which satisfies either of us that she is innocent, neither of us can escape the conclusion that she must have had some knowledge of the occurrence. She has been presented for trial by a jury which, to say the least, was not influenced by anything said by the Government in the favor of the indictment . . . I cannot see how any other course than setting the case down for trial, and trying it will satisfy that portion of the public sentiment, whether favorable to her or not, which is worthy of being respected."

This remarkable letter, so accurate in its prediction, shows how clearly the man best informed understood both the strength and the weakness of the Government's case. The fact that every investigation, so far, had resulted in a decision adverse to the interests of the accused, makes many of the final comments in the newspapers seem absurd. Yet the facts that the evidence was still purely circumstantial; that the unquestioned weapon had not been found; that the absence of blood-stains upon the prisoner's clothing was a telling point in her favor; as well as the difficulty in prevailing upon a jury to convict a woman except upon the most overwhelming proof,—all these points made the District Attorney understand the hopelessness of convicting a defendant whose guilt, he sincerely believed, was nevertheless certain.

Miss Borden was arraigned before Justice Hammond of the Superior Court, in New Bedford, on May 8, when she pleaded to the indictments. Early in the next month she was taken again to the Court House, in the same city, to be put upon her trial. Newspaper readers had almost forgotten her. In the first week in June they were amusing themselves with reports of one of the damage suits of Laidlaw against Russell Sage, for injuries received in the attempt to blow up Mr. Sage. An archaic problem was under debate, whether the World's Fair in Chicago should be opened on Sundays. Lord Dunraven's *Valkyrie* was winning in English waters, and seemed the probable challenger for the *America's* cup. At the end of the week, Edwin Booth died at his home, *The Players*. These far off events were news, during the week that Miss Borden came, as the reporters said, "to face her accusers."

Three judges were on the bench on June 5, 1893, as the trial began. They were Chief Justice Albert Mason and Associate Justices Caleb Blodgett and Justin Dewey. Mr. Knowlton was assisted in the prosecution by the District Attorney for the Eastern District, Mr. William H. Moody. The defence was now entrusted to Mr. George D. Robinson, together with Messrs. Jennings and Adams. Mr. Robinson had been Governor of Massachusetts thrice; he was held in peculiar and unusual esteem by the people of the State for the integrity of his character. The story, then current, that before accepting a retainer in this case he had spent two hours in consultation with Miss Borden in the jail, and that he had come forth declaring his firm belief in her innocence, had done much to hearten her friends and convince the doubtful.

On the first day one hundred and eight talesmen were examined before twelve were selected for the jury. Almost every town and city of the county was represented on this large panel, but not Fall River, and there were no Fall River men on the jury.[6] The fine old question and reply, between the Clerk and the prisoner, have vanished from our courts: "How will you be tried?"

[6] See Appendix for list of jurors.

"By God and my country." "God send you good deliverance!" But Massachusetts keeps some of the ancient phraseology, so after the reading of the indictment, the Clerk said to the jury:

"To each count of which indictment Lizzie Andrew Borden, the prisoner at the bar, has heretofore pleaded and said that thereof she is not guilty, and for trial puts herself upon her country, which country you are. You are now sworn to try the issue. If she is guilty on either or both of said counts, you are to say so, and if she is not guilty on either or both of said counts, you are to say so, and no more. Good men and true, stand fast together and hearken to your evidence."

It is one of the great sensational moments in our civilization: the trial of a woman for her life. The newspapers, for the ultimate thrill, prefer to have a trial for the murder of a lover or a husband, but this was for a crime more rare and terrible,—for parricide. If anybody in the crowded Court, on that warm June day, found the scene dramatic, it was merely because he comprehended its meaning. The proceedings were quiet and dignified, but without ceremony or circumstance; the surroundings were commonplace. There entered no judge in scarlet, acclaimed by trumpeters, as in the trial of Mrs. Maybrick at Liverpool; these justices did not even wear the black silk gowns of our Supreme Court. The sitting was held in a bare, white-walled room, filled with desks, chairs and long settees. Three elderly and bearded gentlemen, with palm-leaf fans, sat a little above the rest, upon the bench. Another beard, a long one, on the chin of the Clerk. Beards, side-whiskers, or heavy moustaches in the jury-box; men still liked to surround their faces with hair. The prisoner came in "walking steadily." She wore a "new dress of black mohair, cut in the latest style, with leg-of-mutton sleeves, which fitted her by no means inferior form to perfection. Upon her head was a jaunty black lace hat trimmed with rosettes of blue velvet and a blue feather . . . She was altogether unembarrassed."

Perhaps the most unusual figures in the New Bedford Court House were the thirty or forty newspaper men from Boston and New York, and from the press associations. They alternately amused and were amused by New Bedford. They sat upon uncomfortable stools and rested their papers upon narrow strips of board, called by courtesy, tables. Writers from the metropolitan journals gave their readers what they were supposed to desire, by describing almost every man in the trial as "stern and Puritanical" and nearly every woman as "an angular old maid." The New Yorker visualizes the inhabitant of New England as looking more or less, in features and costume, like St. Gaudens' statue of Deacon Chapin, "The Puritan," and if, in his expeditions to Newport, Boston or Bar Harbor, he has seen few of this appearance, he clings, nevertheless, to his secret belief.

There may have been women among the reporters; the sob-sister had made her appearance in journalism, and one who signed herself "Amy Robsart" had already written sympathetic articles about Miss Borden languishing in the Taunton jail. Mr. Algernon Blackwood, the novelist, was on the staff of the New York *Sun* at this time, and he refers in his autobiography, "Episodes before Thirty," to the Borden case. His reference indicates more than one lapse of memory. He seems to have talked with the prisoner, but it does not appear whether he was at the trial. None of the bizarre and terrible situations in Mr. Blackwood's stories, with all their appropriate setting, is stranger than the contrast between the homely scene of the Borden house on that August morning and the Æschylean slaughter there enacted. Probably the most distinguished correspondent present was Julian Ralph of the New York *Sun*, although nobody was so conspicuous as Joseph Howard, Jr., of *The New York Recorder* and *The Boston Globe*. At that time many citizens of New England considered it a solemn duty, between breakfast and church on Sunday mornings, to read "Howard's Letter" from New York in the *Globe*. Pontifical in style, and invariably ending with a description, in two words, of the weather in New York, these letters had become a sort of weekly necessity, for reasons difficult to explain today. Mr. Howard had descended upon New Bedford with something of the grandeur of an Oriental embassy, and with every provision for his comfort and convenience. Somehow he secured a chair next the Sheriff, and there, conspicuous in his summer clothes, among all the poor wretches in doleful black, he fairly dominated the scene. Mr. Howard was said to have attended every notable trial in thirty years, including that of Mrs. Surratt of the Lincoln conspiracy.

Before giving any narrative of the progress of the trial, it may be useful to show what the State tried to prove. I will condense into this paragraph and the next an analysis of the case made by Professor Wigmore,[7] author of the "Treatise on Evidence." The State sought to establish that the prisoner had a motive for the crime, and the design to commit it; that she had the opportunity, and the means and the capacity; and finally, that she betrayed consciousness of guilt. The motive was supposed to arise in the family history; in the fact that she was not on good terms with her stepmother; that customarily she and her sister did not eat with the others in the house; and that she had made certain remarks about her stepmother which betrayed her animosity. There was no evidence of design to use an axe, but a general intention to kill was to be shown by the attempt to buy poison. The conversation with Miss Russell on Wednesday night, and the suggestion to Bridget that she go out to buy dress goods, were to support the theory of premeditation.

For opportunity, means and capacity, the State attempted to prove that she had exclusive opportunity; that physically she was not incapable of the deeds; and that one of the hatchets produced in Court—the "handleless" hatchet—was not incapable of being the weapon. Consciousness of guilt, with exclusive opportunity, were the strong points of the prosecution. To establish the former the State relied, first, on the alleged falsehoods to prevent detection of the first death in the story about the note sent to Mrs. Borden. Second, the falsehoods as to the visit to the barn, and the contradictory versions of this story. Third, her knowledge as to the first death. Fourth, her concealment of the knowledge. Fifth, that

[7] See Appendix.

she concealed or destroyed evidence, as will appear in the testimony.

Mr. Moody opened for the Commonwealth. He had begun a career which was to reward him, before middle-age had passed, with two of the great prizes of his profession in America. Of medium-size and sturdy figure, he had a pleasant, youthful countenance, and a manner in public speech of sincere, often intense, conviction, not unlike that of President Roosevelt, whose Cabinet Minister he became. Mr. Moody gave an outline of the history of the case which need not be repeated here, since I have already drawn upon it, as well as other sources. He described the interior of the Borden house,—fortunately this description was supplemented by an inspection, for which the jury were taken to Fall River. One or two points in the address may be mentioned. When he came to the remark which Miss Borden made to her father: "Mrs. Borden has gone out; she had a note from somebody who was sick," he said: "That, gentlemen, we put to you as a lie, intended for no purpose except to stifle inquiry as to the whereabouts of Mrs. Borden." In regard to the stories about the visit to the yard or to the barn, he invited the jury's attention to certain minor differences and to one important discrepancy. To Bridget, to Mrs. Churchill, and to Officer Mullaly, she said that she was in the barn, and came into the house because of a noise she heard. The noise was variously described, to the different persons, as "a groan," "a distress noise" and a "scraping sound."

"All those, gentlemen, you see in substance are stories which include the fact that while she was outside she heard some alarming noise which caused her to rush in and discover the homicide. Well, gentlemen, as inquiry begins to multiply upon her as to her whereabouts, another story comes into view, and she repeats it again and again, and finally repeats it under oath, that at the time, after Bridget went upstairs she went out into the barn to get lead to make sinkers. Now, gentlemen, having in view the character of her statements, that she heard the noise, you will find that when she gave a later and detailed account, she said that she went into the loft of the barn, opened the window, ate some pears up there, and looked over some lead for sinkers, came down, looked into the stove to see if the fire was hot enough that she might go on with her ironing, found it was not, put her hat down, started to go upstairs to await the fire which Bridget was to build for the noonday, and discovered her father. It is not, gentlemen, and I pray your attention to it, a difference of words here. In the one case the statement is that she was alarmed by the noise of the homicide. In the other case, the statement is that she came coolly, deliberately, about her business, looking after her ironing, putting down her hat, and accidentally discovered the homicide as she went upstairs."

Mr. Moody also described other portions of the case for the prosecution, and these may be mentioned as they are reached in the testimony. At the close of his speech, the prisoner fainted. The witnesses first called included Mr. Kieran, the engineer who measured the house; Mr. John Vinnicum Morse; and a number of bank employees and shop-keepers who saw Mr. Borden on the day of his death.

The first important witness was Bridget Sullivan, and her cross-examination by Mr. Robinson seemed to elicit the first bits of information which had not been heard at the preliminary trial. Mr. Robinson dwelt upon the matter of discord in the family. The witness testified that she had never observed any quarrels. Asked the direct question if the daughters came to the table for meals with the rest of the family, the answer was: "No, sir, they did not." The lawyer persisted, and she replied: "Most of the time they did not eat with their father and mother." He suggested that this was because they did not arise as early in the morning, and asked about the custom at dinner. She answered: "Sometimes at dinner; a good many more times they were not." She testified that Miss Lizzie and Mrs. Borden did speak to each other civilly. He asked about the step-daughter's conduct toward Mrs. Borden when the latter was ill, and brought out the disconcerting reply: "I know that she was sick one time, and none of them went into the room while she was sick." He quoted her testimony at the inquest, which was in some degree opposed to this, but did not get her to alter the statement. He returned to the question of their eating together, until she finally said that "they always ate at the same dining-room." He then asked: "Always ate together in the dining-room?" The answer was "Yes." His treatment of the witness on this point seems somewhat disingenuous. Bridget testified that she had no duties in the bed-rooms of the family. The most important points which he brought out in favor of the prisoner were that while Bridget was on the other side of the house, talking with the Kelly's servant, she could not have seen anyone who might have entered the house by the side-yard; and that when she came downstairs, after the murders, she saw no blood on Miss Borden's face or hands. Mr. Robinson touched upon the story of the note to Mrs. Borden, learned that the witness heard the prisoner tell her father that such a note had been received, but then dropped the subject, and did not ask whether the witness had heard of the note from Mrs. Borden, or from anybody except the prisoner. That omission was significant.

Dr. Bowen and Mrs. Churchill followed Bridget Sullivan. All of these witnesses were questioned about the dress which Miss Borden was wearing when they first saw her after the murders. Dr. Bowen's testimony on this point was confused; Mrs. Churchill described it as "a light blue and white ground work . . . with a dark navy blue diamond on it." Shown a dark blue dress, given to the police by the prisoner as the one worn by her that morning, and asked if this was the one she saw, Mrs. Churchill replied: "I did not see her with it on that morning." On cross-examination Mrs. Churchill said that she could not tell much about Bridget's dress on that day; and that she saw no blood on Miss Borden, although she stood over her and had fanned her. Mrs. Churchill also said that Bridget told her the story about the note. The defence promptly tried to clinch this apparently valuable testimony and made the witness repeat it again and again. But on the re-direct examination, Mr. Moody asked:

"Lest there be any mistake, Mrs. Churchill, you don't speak of this talk with Bridget with reference to the note as in substitution, but in addition to what Miss Lizzie Borden told you?"

"It was after Lizzie had told me."

"Then Bridget told you what you have told us?"

"Yes, after that."

When Miss Alice Russell was called, "Miss Borden straightened up in her chair and began to watch the door." Miss Russell entered, and looked, says a reporter, in every direction but toward the prisoner. She related, at length, the conversation with Miss Borden on the night before the murders. When the witness came to relate experiences at the Borden house after the murders, she said that in answer to her question: "What did you go to the barn for, Lizzie?" the answer was: "I went to get a piece of tin or iron to fix my screen." A new and important part of Miss Russell's testimony was that on the Sunday morning after the murders (following Mayor Coughlin's call on Saturday evening) she—the witness—came into the kitchen of the Borden house and saw Miss Lizzie Borden at the stove, with a dress in her hand. Her sister, Miss Emma, asked what she was going to do, and the answer was: "I am going to burn this old thing up; it is covered with paint." Miss Russell left the room without speaking, but on returning saw the prisoner ripping or tearing the garment. She said: "I wouldn't let anybody see me do that, Lizzie." There was no reply. On the next day, Miss Russell said to the prisoner: "I am afraid, Lizzie, the worst thing you could have done was to burn that dress. I have been asked about your dresses." The prisoner answered: "Oh, what made you let me do it? Why didn't you tell me?" This testimony about the dress, said Miss Russell, was not given at the inquest nor at the preliminary trial, nor at her first appearance before the Grand Jury. She further said that the burned dress was a "cheap cotton Bedford cord" with "light blue ground with a dark figure, small figure."

Miss Russell, on cross-examination, said that in the dining-room, on the day of the murder, she found the handkerchiefs that the prisoner had been ironing. Some of them had been ironed; two or three had not. She saw no blood anywhere upon the prisoner. When the dress was burned, on Sunday morning, there was a policeman in the yard at the time. She saw no blood on the dress, and she did not actually see the prisoner put it into the stove.

One of the first of the police witnesses was the assistant city marshal, John Fleet. He had been early to arrive, and to talk with the prisoner. In this conversation she made what was considered a significant remark. In reply to Mr. Fleet's question if she had any idea who could have killed her father and mother, she said: "She is not my mother, sir; she is my stepmother; my mother died when I was a child." One gathers from various sources the impression that there was something in Miss Borden's manner, in all these early interviews, which, as well as the circumstances, tended to arouse suspicion. This, of course, did not reach the jury, but it is often alluded to in contemporary accounts. The cross-examination of Mr. Fleet was long and severe; it was part of the policy of the defence to impeach all the police testimony as incorrect, sometimes deliberately malicious. In the opinion of some of the reporters, the police witnesses were badly confused by Mr. Robinson; this is not apparent in reading the stenographic report. Officer Medley, who arrived at the Borden house at twenty minutes before twelve and heard from Miss Borden about her visit to the barn, promptly went to the place himself. He testified that he especially examined the floor of the loft for foot prints, and found that he could see none. He experimented to see if his own footsteps would be left in the accumulation of dust on the floor, and found that they were.

On the seventh day of the trial, the prosecution offered Miss Borden's own testimony at the inquest, and on Mr. Robinson's objection, argued for its admission, after the jury had withdrawn. Mr. Moody said, without dispute, that the conduct of the inquest had been in accordance with law; that her testimony was not a confession, but rather in the nature of denials, which were evidences of guilt. He made the usual citations of other cases in which similar evidence had been admitted. In reply, Mr. Robinson urged that an accusation had been made against his client, by the Mayor, on August 6, that the inquest was from August 9 to 11, and that from August 6 she was under observation of the police. The house was surrounded. A warrant had been issued—but not served—on August 8; she was arrested, later, under another warrant. She was surrounded by police, a defenceless woman, denied counsel, not told by the Court or the District Attorney that she ought not testify to anything which might incriminate herself. "If that is freedom, God save the Commonwealth of Massachusetts!"

Mr. Moody replied that all this was magnificent, but it was not law. He said that it was agreed that Mr. Jennings did confer with her before she testified, and that it was absurd to suppose that he had not warned her of her rights not to give evidence. The Court withdrew for consultation, and on returning said that Miss Borden was practically under arrest at the time she gave this testimony, and it was therefore excluded.

Doctors Dolan, Wood, and Draper were among the medical witnesses for the State. They were examined and cross-examined at enormous length. They agreed that between one and two hours, probably about one hour and a half, had elapsed between the two deaths,—a fact deduced from the progress of digestion, the warmth of the two bodies, and the condition of the blood from each. A valuable point for the accused woman was made when Professor Wood said that he believed the assailant of Mr. Borden must have been spattered with blood. During the medical testimony the skull of Mr. Borden was produced in court, for purposes of illustration of the nature of the wounds. The mawkish and sentimental newspapers—and this included three-quarters of them at this stage—made great play with this fact, and dwelt upon how it affected the poor prisoner. The newspapers were few which did not act as if the deaths of Mr. and Mrs. Borden ought to have been forgotten long ago; that the officers of the law were little better than brutes to have prosecuted anybody; and that the sole concern of mankind was to rescue, from her grievous position, the "unfortunate girl," and send her home amid a shower of roses.

Mrs. Hannah Gifford, a dress-maker, testified, under objection by the defence, as to a conversation which she had with the prisoner in the month of March, preceding the murders. Mrs. Gifford, in referring to Mrs. Borden had used the word "mother," whereupon Miss Lizzie had said: "Don't say that to me, for she is a mean, good-for-nothing thing." To which the dress-maker: "Oh, Lizzie, you don't mean that?" "Yes, I don't have much to do with her; I stay in my room most of the time." "You come down to your meals, don't you?" "Yes; but we don't eat with them if we can help it."

Miss Anna H. Borden (not a relative) was produced to testify to a similar but milder remark on the ship during the voyage home from Europe, in 1890, but this was excluded as remote. A mass of conflicting evidence surrounded the testimony of Mrs. Hannah Reagan, matron of the Fall River Police Station. She said she overheard a quarrel between the Borden sisters, in which the prisoner said: "Emma, you have given me away, haven't you?" The reply of the elder sister was: "No, Lizzie, I have not." The prisoner answered: "You have; and I will let you see I won't give in one inch." A controversy had arisen over Mrs. Reagan's testimony, and in it were included Mr. Jennings, the police, the Rev. Mr. Buck, and others. At the time the conversation was first reported, in August, a determined attempt was made by Miss Borden's friends to induce Mrs. Reagan to sign a retraction, and thenceforth the incident was like a football, kicked about by the Borden party and the reporters. The original conversation was evidently believed by the prosecution, and was repeated in detail by Mrs. Reagan at the trial. But it was more flatly contradicted than almost any other point in the case for the Government.

The testimony of Eli Bence, as to the poison, was excluded. (See note, in Appendix.) The Government then rested its case.

The defence, to give Professor Wigmore's analysis in one paragraph, did not shake the evidence as to motive. It had excluded the prussic acid evidence. It did not destroy the proof of exclusive opportunity, but it did show that the screen door at the side was not locked at all times. It showed no traces of another person in the house, and only vague reports of others in the vicinity. It failed to prove that the handleless hatchet might not have been used, but tried to suggest that the evidence of the police was wilfully false. It could not shake the story of the note, but suggested that the note might have been part of the murderer's plot. The inconsistent stories about the trip to the barn were attributed to excitement, and the most damaging of them—the inquest testimony—was excluded. It was shown that lead was found in the barn loft, but no fish-line was produced, and no screen in need of repair was identified. "The inconsistent stories as to her return and discovery of the murder were in part slid over, in part ignored, and in part discredited." The stronghold of the defence was the utter absence of blood-stains on the person of the accused. Five or six persons saw her within ten minutes, and saw no stains on her. "It is safe to say that this was the decisive fact of the case."

Mr. Jennings opened for the defence. He dwelt upon the fact that not one particle of direct evidence had been produced against her. He quoted cases to show the unreliability of circumstantial evidence,—always an effective argument, for although attorneys may argue and judges expound until the end of time, two or three persons out of five will still be found saying: "I don't believe in circumstantial evidence." He pointed out that the Government, for all the array of axes and hatchets they brought into Court, were not positive about any one of them. He denied the proof of exclusive opportunity. He asserted that others had been in the barn before Medley paid his visit.

The defence had little need of any witnesses. The previous good character of the prisoner had been conceded by the Government, so no testimony was offered on that point. A number of witnesses did appear; they were solemnly heard, and duly cross-examined; but at this distance they appear in no other light than as comic relief. Two ladies, neighbors of the Bordens, named Chagnon, testified that they had heard a thumping sound in the direction of the Borden barn, the night before the murders. (It had been investigated, and shown to be dogs upsetting barrels of waste to get at some bones. Even had it been other than this, did the defence suggest that the murderer, arriving twelve hours in advance of the crime, had taken up quarters in the barn—perhaps to get an early chance at the sinkers—and had announced his coming by thumping on the floor?) One Mrs. Durfee had heard a man, a year before, make threats against Mr. Borden; her testimony was excluded as remote. One or two witnesses appeared to tell of a drunken man seen sitting on the Borden steps, the night before. Dr. Handy described his Wild Eyed Man,—not satisfied that he was "Mike the Soldier." The appearance of Hyman Lubinsky, an ice-cream peddler, gave an exotic flavor to the day's proceedings. He had driven through Second Street at some time that morning, when he "saw a lady come out the way from the barn to the stairs from the back of the house." This was offered in corroboration of the story of the visit to the barn, but it was discarded testimony, as he had already been carefully examined by the Government, and his idea of time shown to be faulty. The Clan Lubinsky were more of a novelty in 1893 than today, and Hyman's tart answers to the District Attorney ("What has a person got eyes for, but to look with?") must have amused the auditors.

Better still were a pair of youthful witnesses, Everett Brown and Thomas Barlow, a couple of boys who had apparently determined to get into Court one way or another. The spirit of romance burned in them, a far hotter flame than their passion for fact. They had not had, like Huck Finn and Tom Sawyer, the luck to witness a murder, and to be able to take a solemn oath by midnight. But they did about as well. They ate their dinners at the surprising hour of 10.30 A.M., on August 4, and arrived at the scene almost before the crime was committed.

"We went in the side gate."

"You say 'we.' Who?"

"Me and Brownie."

They went up in the barn-loft far ahead of anybody else, although they paused a while at the stairs, and dared each other to go first, each thinking that "somebody might drop an axe on him." They enjoyed the loft because it was "cooler" up there than it was outdoors. The District Attorney was inhospitable toward these fairy-tales.

"The barn loft was a nice, comfortable, cool place?"

"Yes, sir."

They had approached the Borden house "fooling along," and they were asked what that meant.

"He was pushing me off the sidewalk and I was pushing him off."

Ah, "me and Brownie," the rest of the folk who were in the New Bedford Court House, that day, are either dead, or else they are old, old people. But you are not too old to recall with delight the day you had a trip over from Fall River, and a free ride on the train, chummed with the police, and for a while stood with the fierce light of publicity beating upon you, the reporters taking down your words, to be printed that evening in all the papers. What if the Goddess who lives in a well, blushed and turned aside while you spoke?

Joseph Lemay from Steep Brook, led forward the murderer of melodrama. On August 16, on a farm four miles from the city, he was in a deep wood, a savage place, holy and enchanted. Suddenly he heard a voice thrice repeating the words: "Poor Mrs. Borden!" He looked over a wall and saw a man sitting on the ground. The man picked up a hatchet and shook it at him. Then he—the man with the hatchet—leaped over the wall and disappeared; he had spots of blood on his shirt. The Court, however, did not let Mr. Lemay entertain the jury with this anecdote. It was unnecessary; the Court were to do far better for the prisoner than all these romantics combined.

Miss Emma Borden was one of the last witnesses for the defence, and she bore with composure a long and skilful cross-examination. She was not allowed by the Court to tell about the custom in the family of burning old dresses. She admitted that there had been trouble between her father and stepmother on one side, and her sister and herself on the other. She said that it was the prisoner, not herself, who had become reconciled with the stepmother, and the statement was considered both gallant and sisterly.

The prisoner did not testify in her own defence. The jury were, of course, duly informed that she was within her rights in refraining from the witness stand, and the Justice who delivered the charge gave a long explanation of why she might refrain. They were warned not to consider it as telling against her. But we, who are not jurymen, may wonder at it. She was not a foreigner, unable to speak or understand the language, nor a timid or feeble person, who could not make a calm appearance. She had not an evil record in her past life, which might be disclosed in cross-examination, unfairly to prejudice the jury. The spotlessness of her life was acclaimed by her defenders. She was known to have made the most unaccountable and contradictory statements about her actions at the time of her father's murder. Here was her chance to explain them all away. She did not accept it. None of the warm admirers who were soon to throng around her, or to fill the mails and the wires with enthusiastic messages of congratulation, ever seemed to notice the fact. The law, in their opinion, owed her an abject apology for having suspected her. At the close of the arguments, and before the charge, the Chief Justice informed her that it was her privilege to speak in person to the jury. Secure from question, she arose and repeated the thirteen words in which her counsel had coached her:

"I am innocent. I leave it to my counsel to speak for me."

On the twelfth day of the trial Mr. Robinson made the final argument for his client. One gathers from reading it, that, like his conduct of the case, it was marked by courtesy, and even more by kindliness, and a manner of transparent honesty which did not have to be assumed. The advocate was held in entire respect everywhere in the State. He was addressing a jury chiefly from the country, or from small towns and villages, and he never failed to put himself in sympathy with them. Although he had dwelt in the tents of wickedness long enough to study at Harvard, to serve in the State Legislature in Boston, and for three years as Governor of the Commonwealth, and although he had even been in Washington for a number of years, as a Member of Congress, he never failed to drop a hint as to what he thought of city folks, or about the general superiority of men who lived on farms.

He described the murders as terrible and revolting beyond all imagination,—so terrible that they could only be the work of a maniac, a fiend, a devil. Such acts were morally and physically impossible for the prisoner at the bar. In the days following the murders the police had been criticized for not catching somebody; they had perforce to go out and make an arrest. Once having done this, they easily persuaded themselves of the prisoner's guilt. The prosecution had said that she was in the house on that morning. Well, that was a proper place for her to be. Did they wish her to be out on the street? It was where he would wish his daughter to be; at home. He made a strong argument against the contention that she necessarily would have seen the body of her stepmother from the hall at the head of the stairs, or from the stairs while descending. He said that *Bridget*, as well as Miss Borden, had been told by Mrs. Borden about the note. Mr. Robinson's words were:

"Both Bridget and Lizzie had learned from Mrs. Borden that she had had a note. Mrs. Borden had told Lizzie. Mrs. Borden had told Bridget. She had given Bridget the work to do, washing the windows. She said to her: 'I have got a note to go out and see some one that was sick.' "

On this point, Professor Wigmore writes: "The only blot upon an almost perfectly conducted trial was the attempt of the counsel for the defence in argument to show that the information as to the note emanated originally from Bridget, and that the accused merely repeated it. This was decidedly a breach of propriety, because it was not merely an argument suggesting the fair possibility of that explanation, but a distinct assertion that the testimony was of that purport, and therefore, in effect, a false quotation of the testimony. In truth, the accused's statement about the note was her own alone and was one of the points to be explained."

Mr. Robinson suggested that the note might have been

a part of the scheme of the murderer to get Mrs. Borden out of the house, or otherwise to entrap her. He made light of the supposed discomforts of the Borden home, and of the plain fare served at their table. He held the array of hatchets up to ridicule. In ending he asked for a prompt verdict of " 'not guilty' that she may go back and be Lizzie Andrew Borden of Fall River in that blood-stained and wrecked home, where she has passed her life so many years."

Mr. Knowlton, in closing for the Government, had a much harder problem. He was asking for the conviction of a woman, and a church member, who was supported and buttressed by friends, and by a press which had almost ceased to do anything except palpitate to the sentimentalism of the noisier section of the public. He was a thickset man, with a tenacious manner, easily exaggerated by his detractors into the air of the inquisitor or the tyrant. No prosecuting officer in Massachusetts ever had a less enviable task than his; none ever carried his work through with more ability or more courageous fulfillment of a public duty. His address was acknowledged, even in the hostile press, as far abler than that of his opponent. Mr. Robinson talked down to the whims and prejudices of a country jury; Mr. Knowlton talked straight to citizens whom he assumed had an eye to their duty. He argued that neither church membership nor the fact of being a woman were proof against guilt.

> With all sympathy for the woman, in which, believe me, I share with you; with all distrust of any

evidence until it is brought home to your convictions, in which you will let me share with you, and all good and true men; with due regard, if you please, to the consequences of your action, yet let me remind you that you stand not only to deliver that woman but to deliver the community. It was a crime which may well challenge your most sober and sacred attention. That aged man, that aged woman, had gone by the noonday of their lives. They had borne the burden and heat of the day. They had accumulated a competency which they felt would carry them through the waning years of their lives, and hand in hand they expected to go down to the sunset of their days in quiet and happiness. But for that crime they would be enjoying the air of this day. But for that assassin many years of their life, like yours, I hope, sir, would have been before them, when the cares of life are past, when the anxieties of their daily avocations had ceased to trouble them, and together they would have gone down the hill of life, serene in an old age which was happy because the happiness had been earned by a life of fidelity and toil.

Over those bodies we stand, Mr. Foreman. We sometimes forget the past. Over those bodies we stand, and we say to ourselves, is it possible that this crime cannot be discovered? You are standing as has been suggested, in the presence of death itself. It is not only what comes hereafter, but it is the double death that comes before. There is a place, it is the chamber of death, where all these personal animosities, passions, and prejudices, have no room, where all matters of sentiment are aside, where nothing but the truth, the naked truth, finds room and lodgment. In that spirit I adjure you to enter upon the trial of this case. It is the most solemn duty of your lives.

Illustrations of circumstantial evidence have often been given in court, from Thoreau's playful remark about a trout in the milk, to the more familiar one of footprints. Perhaps it has seldom been more effectively presented than in Mr. Knowlton's speech:

> What is called sometimes circumstantial evidence is nothing in the world but that presentation of circumstances—it may be one or fifty—there isn't any chain about it—the word "chain" is a misnomer as applied to it; it is the presentation of circumstances from which one is irresistibly driven to the conclusion that crime has been committed. Talk about a chain of circumstances! When that solitary man had lived on his island for twenty years and believed that he was the only human being there, and that the cannibals and savages that lived around him had not found him, nor had not come to his island, he walked out one day on the beach, and there he saw the fresh print in the sand of a naked foot. He had no lawyer to tell him that that was nothing but a circumstance. He had no distinguished counsel to urge upon his fears that there was no chain about that thing which led him to a conclusion. His heart beat fast; his knees shook be-

neath him, he fell to the ground in fright, because Robinson Crusoe knew when he saw that circumstance that a man had been there that was not himself. It was circumstantial evidence; it was nothing but circumstantial evidence, but it satisfied him.

The District Attorney emphasized the pre-decease of Mrs. Borden as the key to the case, since the murderer of Mr. Borden was also the murderer of Mrs. Borden. No outsider could have planned it, nor lurked about the house to execute it. Mrs. Borden, he said, had no outside enemies. These men with a grudge against her husband had no grudge against her. He touched upon Mrs. Gifford's testimony, and upon the prisoner's promptness in saying to the officer: "She is not my mother." He refused to withdraw, but re-affirmed Mr. Moody's statement that the story about the note was a lie. "No note came; no note was written; nobody brought a note; nobody was sick . . . I will stake the case on your belief or disbelief in the truth or falsity of that proposition." He disputed Mr. Robinson's claim that Bridget said she had heard about the note from Mrs. Borden. Mr. Knowlton met the argument that the prisoner had no quarrel with her father by asserting that when Mrs. Borden had been killed, it became apparent to her that she must kill Mr. Borden too, in order to save herself from his accusation. Her father was the one person who would be in no doubt who was guilty, as he knew who hated the step-mother. The prosecutor dwelt upon the absurdity of the stay in the barn-loft on so hot a day.

The defence, he said, could introduce evidence about dogs upsetting ash-barrels, why did they not explain what screen needed repair, and why did they not produce the fish-line for which sinkers were required? The prisoner's coolness was touched upon; she did not rush out of the house, nor send for police; she sent only for her friends; and public knowledge of the murders came by accident. On the difficulty of the blood-stains upon her clothing, he reasoned that she had ample opportunity to remove the stains of the first murder. As for the second, he acknowledged the difficulty of the question. "I cannot answer it. You cannot answer it." He did draw attention, however, to the roll of paper seen in the stove, which might have been used for protection; and to the murdered man's coat, not hanging on a hook, but folded at the head of the couch where he lay. That also might have been used as a shield.[8] The question about the dresses was debated at great length by both counsel. The prosecution contended that, at all events, the one produced by the prisoner was not the one worn on that morning. It was silk; an unlikely material for morning housework.

The charge to the jury was given by Mr. Justice Dewey. It became the subject of a great amount of discussion, and the mildest comment is that it was extremely favorable to the prisoner. Mr. Howard, the newspaper correspondent, and by this time one of the warmest of Miss Borden's sympathizers, called it "a plea for the innocent," a description which could hardly have been

[8] There had been no Sherlock Holmes to look at that coat and see if it had spatters of blood *inside* its folds.

enjoyed by the learned and supposedly impartial judge who delivered it. Criticism of the charge is too delicate a task for a layman, even a layman who has already floundered so far into legal waters that he feels like the judge, who, suddenly called upon for the first time in his life to preside at an admiralty case, began by murmuring:

> And may there be no moaning of the bar,
> When I put out to sea.

At twenty-four minutes past three, on the afternoon of June 20, the thirteenth day of the trial, the jury went out. They stayed a little over an hour, or until about half-past four. At that time, they came in with the verdict of "not guilty." *The Boston Journal*, which was favorable to Miss Borden, said that two ballots were taken and that on the first ballot one juror voted for conviction. It is usually said, however, that they were agreed from the start, and that they stayed out an hour only to avoid suspicion of not having considered the Government's case.

The familiar scene was enacted,—cheers, tears, congratulations; hand-shakings and thanks for each of the jury-men,—all a matter of course as long ago as when Mark Twain and C. D. Warner wrote the court scene in "The Gilded Age." Mr. Howard had a few words of felicitation for the heroine, and received her thanks, as he modestly records in both his papers. It was a privilege to shake her hand. Mrs. Livermore and Mrs. Fessenden were in raptures; they wired congratulations, and spoke of the District Attorney and other officers of the Government in terms of severe condemnation. The impression given by the newspapers is that it was a popular outcome. *The Boston Journal* said that the verdict "saves from deadly peril and vindicates from cruel suspicion a true, modest, and upright woman." The same paper had published a poll of citizens of New England as to whether the case were "proven" or "not proven." Persons were consulted in many of the larger towns, and there was a strong majority for "not proven." *The Boston Globe* agreed with the verdict; *The Boston Herald* was neutral, and said that the evidence was insufficient. *The Boston Post* criticized the Government. *The Springfield Republican*, which in the early days of the case had taken a severe line with the police, was less outspoken, and intimated that many persons would still believe her guilty. Another paper of more than ordinary merit, *The Providence Journal*, said that many would find the verdict unsatisfactory. *The Fall River Globe*, which firmly supported the police and the case of the Government (and never ceased to do so) suggested that there were many in Fall River who would not agree with the jury,—a very sound prediction, and one which has not been falsified in thirty years.

But if the press of New England were not absolutely unanimous in throwing their hats into the air, and cheering for the defendant, that of New York had no such hesitation. *The New York Herald* said: "It will be the verdict of the great public." The *Herald* held a poll of lawyers all over the country, and these almost unanimously voted the case of the State as "not proven," although here and there a lawyer said that he believed in the defendant's guilt, but did not expect a conviction. *The World* said: "No other verdict could have been expected"; it had protested against the indictment; the trial was merely an instance of "police blundering," and in the meanwhile the real culprit had escaped. The *Tribune* remarked that: "The New Bedford jury have done what they could to restore Lizzie Borden to her rightful place in a world of hope and happiness." The advantage was all with the State in the final arguments; Knowlton's speech was much superior to Robinson's. "We have no hesitation in pronouncing this a righteous verdict." The cynical will say that it is a Scotch verdict of "not proven," but the *Tribune* cried out against such injustice. It remained for the usually sober *New York Times* to reach the heights of ecstasy. The verdict, according to that paper, was "a certain relief to every rightminded man and woman." The *Times* spoke of "this most unfortunate and cruelly persecuted woman. . . ." "There was never any serious reason to suppose that she was guilty." The result was "a condemnation of the police authorities of Fall River and of the legal officers who secured the indictment and have conducted the trial." It had been "a shame to Massachusetts." The article, filling half a column on the editorial page, varies from severity toward the law officers to touching sympathy for Miss Borden; it condemns the conduct of the former as "outrageous"; they were "guilty of a barbarous wrong to an innocent woman and a gross injury to the community." It is a misfortune that she has not legal recourse against them and a means of bringing them to account. "Her acquittal is only a partial atonement for the wrong that she has suffered." The police force of Fall River is denounced as the "usual inept and stupid and muddle-headed sort." If the writer for the *Times* had never read a word of evidence on the case, and had turned for his information to some especially lachrymose sob-sister, who, like some of Miss Borden's friends in Court, held their hands over their ears when anything was uttered against her, this article might be explained.

None of this means to say that, on the case as it was presented to the jury, a verdict of "guilty" was to be expected. Few lawyers have been willing to assert that the result was against the weight of evidence. *The New York Recorder*, for which Mr. Howard wrote his letters, tried the case in its columns more frankly than any of the other papers, and actually organized a "special jury" of more or less distinguished citizens, whose pictures were printed in a row every day.[9] They were furnished verbatim reports of each day's proceedings, and on the last day of all were asked to vote "proven" or "not proven." This "jury" included the Rev. Dr. Edward Everett Hale, William Sulzer, Samuel Gompers, George Fred Williams, DeLancey Nicoll, Lucy Stone, and Albert A. Pope, and these with the other five, all voted "not proven." The latitude of the Scotch verdict must have been a relief to such an experienced attorney as Mr. Nicoll.

After the newspaper comments, it is instructive to read a few passages from two articles on the case, both written by lawyers, who were moreover conversant with all the evidence. They are the only serious discussions which I

[9] This was probably repeated in *The Boston Globe.*

have seen. Mr. Wigmore, in the *American Law Review* [10] said:

> It is difficult to see how the assailant could have avoided receiving blood-marks during the assaults; it is also difficult to understand what arrangements of implements and clothing, and what combinations of opportunity, suffered to allow the accused, if she was the assailant, to remove the traces upon weapon and clothes after each assault. But, first, these are difficulties of ignorance; in other words, there is no proved fact which is inconsistent with the thing being so; we merely cannot find traces of the exact *modus operandi;* second, this difficulty is equally as great for any other person than the accused, and we may say greater; it is a difficulty that cannot change the balance of conviction. On the other hand, the conduct of the accused after the killing was such that no conceivable hypothesis except that of guilt, will explain the inconsistencies and improbabilities that were asserted by her. The statements about the purpose of the barn visit, and about the discovery of the father's death, are frightfully inconsistent; while the story of the note requires for its truth a combination of circumstances almost inconceivable. We may add to this the inevitable query, Why did the accused not take the stand to explain these things? Of course, it was her legal right to remain silent; but the rule against self-crimination is not one of logic or of relevancy; it is a rule of

[10] See Appendix.

> policy and fairness, based on broad considerations of average results desirable in the long run. It cannot prevent us as logical beings, from drawing our inferences; and if we weigh in this case the confounding inconsistencies and improbabilities of these statements and then place with these the opportunity and the refusal to explain them, we cannot help feeling that she failed to explain them because she could not; and one side of the balance sinks heavily.
>
> This is not saying that the evidence justified a conviction. . . .

On the rulings of the Court, Mr. Wigmore almost invariably disagrees. "It may be suggested . . . with all deference, that . . . most of what was excluded seems admissible." On the prussic acid evidence the Court decided that the evidence did not come up to the offer. "As for the authorities . . . the clear result is for the admission of the evidence." On the question of admitting the inquest statement, Mr. Wigmore adopts Mr. Moody's argument; that there was no doubt that Mr. Jennings informed his client of her rights, "and that he allowed her to go on the stand because he deliberately concluded that it was the best policy for her, by so doing, to avoid all appearance of concealment or guilt. And yet the ruling of the Court allowed them to blow hot and cold,—to go on the stand when there was something to gain and to remain silent when the testimony proved dangerous to use."

The Court ruled against the defence when it proposed to prove the family custom of burning old dresses, and this, Mr. Wigmore believes, would have over-turned the verdict if it had resulted in a conviction. He further said that the charge that the police showed a spirit of persecution was "utterly unjustifiable."

Judge Charles G. Davis of Plymouth, wrote to *The Boston Advertiser*, letters afterwards published as "The Conduct of the Law in the Borden Case."[11] They contain the severest criticisms of the rulings by the Court, and leave no manner of doubt that the author thought that these decisions led to a grave error. The ruling about the poison "was received with almost universal surprise by the bar." On that which excluded the inquest testimony he remarks: "It is difficult to see how Miss Borden was under arrest when she was not under arrest." Judge Davis's analysis of the evidence is an extremely interesting consideration of the laws of chance and of averages to show the improbability or impossibility of the murders having been committed by a person from outside the house. "It is a rule of law that the possession of property recently stolen and unaccounted for is sufficient for conviction. . . . But the same law . . . applies to capital crimes. Here was a person who had in possession the bodies of two victims robbed of the precious jewels of their lives. Does anybody think that if this evidence had been applied to a case of robbery, or of mere property, the law administered or the verdict would have been the same?"

In the charge of the judge, writes Judge Davis, the justice went beyond his legitimate function with respect to matters of fact. On the charge and on the rulings,

[11] See Appendix.

Judge Davis says in his second letter: "It was not the prisoner, but the Commonwealth which did not have a fair trial." Was Mr. Justice Dewey's "the tone of a judge or of an advocate?" Here the author referred to such words in the charge as this: "Is it reasonable and credible that she could have killed Mrs. Borden at or about the time claimed by the Government . . . ?"

It is impracticable to quote more, but I am led to believe, from conversations with lawyers, that the Superior Court of Massachusetts has never been subjected to such criticism as that resulting from the conduct of its justices in the Borden case. And in this criticism, there was no hint or intimation of corruption, but of a mental infirmity or bias resulting from an unwillingness to believe that a woman could murder her father.

The sense of outrage felt by a considerable portion of the community becomes apparent in the extraordinary series of articles published annually, for many years, in *The Fall River Globe.* These always appeared about August 4, the anniversary of the murders, and were very pointed, to say the least. Thus, on August 4, 1904, an article one and a half columns long is headed: "A Dozen Years Since the Bordens Were Brutally Butchered. Perhaps Murderer or Murderess May Be in the City. Who Can Tell?" It says that the police were abused, although they made up their minds correctly within forty-eight hours "as to the dastard." It jeers at the story of the "Wild Eyed Man," and the Portuguese farm laborer, and the man with the grudge against Andrew Borden, "and Lubinsky," "and me and Brownie," "and the sinkers in the barn loft and all the rest of the rot and nonsense that ran riot through the disordered imagination of a prejudiced and gullible public . . . Who knows, even now, that the vile minded murderer, may not be at large in the community, walking, stalking or driving about in carriage or car . . . ? Perhaps the good people of Fall River may be daily meeting him—or her—in hall, store, or railroad train . . ." The "man—or woman" "he—or she" "him—or her" *motif* recurs throughout.

On August 4th, 1905 a less indignant article has the caption: "Great Wrong is Righted after 13 Years of Misrepresentation. No Murders were Committed On August 4, 1892. Despite the Belief that Andrew and Abby Borden Died in that Manner." There follow nearly two columns of sarcasm, ending:

> There were No Borden Murders!
> Both the Victims of 13 Years Ago
> Died as the Result of Excessive Heat!

This persecution of the "unfortunate girl" was probably resented by the Borden party in Fall River, but nothing seems to have been done about it. It is one of the oddities of the case that once the acquittal was secured the Borden party began to melt and disintegrate.

There is a persistent belief that the case has figured in fiction, and that more than one novelist has drawn upon it for a plot. Of no other American murder, so far as I am aware, is this so often said. There is a noticeable fact about real crimes when they are put into novels or stories; they appear in the fictitious form so altered as to be almost unrecognizable. The writer has merely borrowed a hint, if anything, from the supposed source. The tale most frequently mentioned as based upon the Fall River murders is Miss Mary Wilkins's prize story, "The Long Arm," but it really contains hardly as much of the case as an analytical chemist would call a "trace." A woman is accused of killing somebody, but she is, of course, triumphantly innocent. Much nearer to the real thing are a few sentences in "The Summit House Mystery, or The Earthly Purgatory," by Lily Dougall (1905). The author, a native of Canada, but living in England, had apparently slight acquaintance with the United States. She had heard something about the Borden case. The scene of her story is Georgia, and there is simply a brief reference to "Mr. Claxton and his second wife" who were "suddenly killed." It appeared that "a large body of circumstantial evidence proved that Hermione," his daughter, "was alone in the house with them." Hermione, needless to say, is quite innocent.[12]

Miss Borden's name appeared again in the newspapers in February 1897, about three and a half years after the acquittal. On the 16th and 17th of that month, articles were printed in *The Providence Journal*, the first being headed: "Lizzie Borden Again. A Warrant for her Arrest issued from a local Court. Two Paintings Missed from Tilden-Thurber Co.'s Store. Said to Have Been Traced to Miss Borden's Home in Fall River." In the warrant, according to the second article, she was charged with larceny of a painting on porcelain, called "Love's Dream." "It is known," said the *Journal*, "that the

[12] There are four pages (fact, not fiction) about the Borden case in John Elfreth Watkins's *Famous Mysteries*. (Philadelphia, 1919.)

warrant was issued. It was never served and it is said that the two paintings are still in the possession of Miss Lizzie Borden." The articles are long, and the little which was known was discussed fully. The incident attracted much attention in Fall River. The Tilden-Thurber Corporation, a firm of silversmiths and jewellers in Providence, write (1924) "We have no records regarding the Lizzie Borden case but our recollection of the situation is that the warrant for arrest was based on shoplifting episodes which were finally adjusted."

At a later date, Miss Nance O'Neil, the distinguished actress, was involved in financial difficulties and litigation with her managers and creditors. These took the form of hearings in the equity session at the Court in Boston. Miss Borden emerged from her retirement and became an almost daily spectator at the trial. Since she can hardly have been amused by the legal proceedings, it is supposed that the attraction lay in the interest she felt for Miss O'Neil as an artist, for the latter was a tragedian of great ability.

The closing appeal in Mr. Robinson's final address to the jury has not been fulfilled with precision. He asked that she might go back "and be Lizzie Andrew Borden of Fall River" in her old home. Miss Borden now lives about a mile and a half from her old home, and her name appears in the telephone directory as Lizbeth A. Borden. She is not often seen in public. Her house is spacious enough for a family of ten; a gray building in modified Queen Anne type of architecture, by no means in bad taste. A touch of romance appears, in the name *Maplecroft*, in raised letters on one of the stone steps. The street is pleasant, and the houses are fairly large, with lawns and gardens. The window shades of *Maplecroft* are methodically drawn down to the middle-sash, while white curtains screen the panes. There is a large glass sun-porch, also well-curtained. The big garage, at the rear of the lawn, has an extravagant amount of plate glass set in its doors and windows. The garden accessories include a sun-dial on the lawn, while thoughtfulness for small creatures is manifested in a green bird-house in one of the trees. It is a generous bird-house; no mere box for a pair of wrens, but one capable of sheltering families of blue-birds, if they care for it.

Miss Emma Borden is no longer with her sister. They separated a number of years ago, when the elder lady went first to Fairhaven—where she had been on that famous 4th of August—and then to Providence, to live. On May 11, 1923, the newspapers recorded that Miss Lizzie Borden was engaged in litigation with her sister. There was a disagreement between them about the sale of the A. J. Borden building on South Main Street, owned jointly by the two. The younger desired to sell her share, but the elder objected. Hence a petition in probate, filed by Miss Lizzie, or Lizbeth, seeking an equal distribution of the property.

Few others of the participants in the trial are left. When Mr. Jennings died, in 1923, there were no others of the justices or the counsel living. Perhaps, on a farm in Seekonk, or another of those little villages, lingers some member of the jury which for thirteen days endured all that examination of expert, and other, witnesses; and then when they had received the thanks of the lady they had freed, stayed not a moment, but (to the great delight of Julian Ralph) strode right across the market-place to the nearest hotel-bar, and (still acting in unison) drowned the dreadful thirst which had so long accumulated. I have read of one jury—I am not sure if it was this one—who were deprived, by some severe sheriff, of the consolation of tobacco, during their long confinement. Perhaps the idea was that by making men uncomfortable you enable them to arrive at the truth.

Those who remember the murders in 1892, and the trial in 1893, sometimes enjoy raking up the old embers, and recalling the days when families bickered about the case over the dinner table; when husbands and wives parted in wrath after breakfast, and met again at evening to take up the controversy once more. The fact that the plot of "Edwin Drood" is never to be solved, makes the book exasperating to some readers, but highly fascinating to others. There are, in the Borden mystery, a dozen unanswered questions to ponder. What was the meaning of the laugh from the head of the stairs, heard by Bridget Sullivan? What is the explanation of the burglary, in 1891? What caused the mysterious illness in the family? Assuming the theory of an assassin from outside, where did he go? What did he do with the weapon? What was his motive? Why did he kill Mrs. Borden? Adopting the opinion of the prosecution, how could the departure of Bridget, to her own room, be counted upon? Or the time of Mr. Morse's return? What was the truth about the poison story?

Could anybody have made this attempt so openly? (The answer is that such things have often been done.) Were there any grounds for the suspicions entertained against two men, and at least one other woman, all of whom testified at the trial? (Suspicions, that is, of complicity.) Will the whole truth ever come out?

# THE TWENTY-THIRD STREET MURDER

## THE TWENTY-THIRD STREET MURDER

MISS FLORA M'FLIMSEY of Madison Square is by far the most celebrated resident upon its borders. She was the mere fanciful creation of a maker of *vers de société*, but the name of the park upon which she lived follows more trippingly on the tongue after her fluffy appellation, than after the sober name of any of the veritable statesmen and merchants whose home actually stood in that once fashionable section. It was 1857 when the world first learned about the distressing condition of the M'Flimsey wardrobe. If the lady looked out through her tears, and through the windows of her father's house, she saw a broken sky-line, it is true, but not as it is to-day, broken by towers of varying height, by buildings square and buildings triangular. What she saw was the gap of an occasional vacant lot which interrupted the uniform rows of dwellings, three or four storeys high. The park was leafy, as it is now, but I think it was also rather more given to thick bushes near the ground. The Fifth Avenue Hotel was soon to rise, at the corner of West Twenty-third Street, to the surprising altitude of six storeys, but to be equipped, so it was rumored, with a new contrivance called an "elevator."

The thirteen years which followed Miss M'Flimsey's appearance were eventful, and often exciting, in New York. Broadway and Madison Square heard the tramp of soldiers, going to the war. An Admiral and a Cabinet Minister gained the reputations which ensured that years later they should be set up in bronze at corners of the park. The only monument in Flora's day was that shaft to Major-General Worth, over whose bones thousands of persons now walk daily, without the remotest notion that anybody at all is buried there. The dedication of his monument took place in the very year of Miss M'Flimsey's betrothal, and—if she could find anything to wear—she was doubtless present, to the distraction of the officers of the Seventh Regiment, which formed the guard of honor.

But for thirteen years and many more the office-buildings and the sky-scraping towers came not; the neighborhood was residential, innocent, quietly fashionable. The region was "uptown," and in 1870 the *New York Herald* could find it in its heart to refer to Madison Square and West Twenty-third Street as "aristocratic purlieus."

West Twenty-third was a street of private residences, equipped with the high stoops of New York tradition, and built of the brown stone which reduced many parts of the city to a gloomy chocolate color. The side-walks were broad, and there were trees, which for a week or two in the spring were the haunt of measuring-worms. These worms fell upon and annoyed the ladies and gentlemen who passed along the side-walks, until somebody sought a remedy, and with happy inspiration, imported the English sparrow. (An Englishman once assured me, with meaning in his tone, that this sparrow is both decorous and gentlemanly when at home; he turns into a bounder only on coming to "the States.") The folk who dodged the measuring-worms upon Twenty-third Street in the summer of 1870 would have been beyond my power to visualize, except for the fact that twenty-one or two years ago my heart and the heart of every undergraduate of my time was thrilled by the delicious spectacle of Miss Ethel Barrymore as *Mme. Trentoni* in Clyde Fitch's comedy, "Captain Jinks." The scene was New York in the early 1870's, and in the book of the play one may see the flounces and furbelows of the ladies, the braid-bordered coats, low-crowned bowler hats, and the luxurious whiskers of the young gentlemen, worn at the time when Horace Greeley was trying to replace General Grant in the White House.

Life was pleasant, life was gay in that warm summer of 1870. The New Yorker neither knew nor cared that the city was being systematically robbed of millions upon millions. The *Times*, *Harper's Weekly*, and Thomas Nast had not yet begun the attack which later was to drive forth Tweed and his rascals. A. Oakey Hall was mayor—"elegant Oakey"—Nast called him O. K. Haul. He appears, well to the front, in the most celebrated cartoon—except one—in American political caricature: Nast's "Who Stole the People's Money? 'Twas Him!" Mayor Hall is the bearded person with the drooping *pince-nez*, next but one to the great chief in that dismal ring. The newspaper reader, about the middle of July, found something more exciting than the doings of President Grant and his Cabinet; war was breaking out in Europe. Prussian diplomatists, less clumsy than in our time, had maneuvered France into declaring the war which they had planned and desired. American opinion at first favored Germany; there was little cause, in this country, to love Napoleon III, after his attitude in our Civil War, and after his Mexican adventure which had ended but a few years before. The Prussian, however, was running true to form; there were bitter complaints in the Berlin papers against "English neutrality." The English, it seemed, were selling cartridges to the French, and that, as everyone knew who lived under the protection of the good old German Gott, was quite wicked. One is hopeless in international politics who does not understand that Germany may make war on anybody, may sell munitions to anybody, or buy them from anybody. But when any of these things are done by one of Germany's foes, or to the advantage of one of her foes, the case is different, culture is betrayed, and it is proper to whine.

By the last week in July the weather was intolerably hot. "Everybody" (five or ten per cent of the population) was out of town. A private citizen from Mississippi, Mr. Jefferson Davis, was on his way to New York, in order to sail for England on the Cunarder *Russia.* Few of the theaters were open. At Wallack's, Emmet was appearing in "Fritz; our Cousin German." At the Grand Opera House, Twenty-third Street and Eighth Avenue (James Fisk, Jr., Proprietor, —a year or two from Stokes's bullet) was Kathi Lanner and her "Viennoise Ballet and Pantomime Troupe." Josie Mansfield's name does not appear in the advertisements. And the Booth Theater was to reopen on August 15th with Mr. Joseph Jefferson as *Rip Van Winkle.*

On July 28th, hoping for some relief from the heat, New York watched the thunder clouds in the sky, and waited for the storm which hovered near all day. The early evening was pleasant, and the desired rain did not come until about ten o'clock, but then it came with terrific force. At eight or nine, ladies and gentlemen could still be abroad in the streets, without danger of getting wet. At ten o'clock there was a downpour of rain for an hour or two, and, as in the stage directions for the first scene of Macbeth: thunder and lightning. The incessant crashes wakened folk who had gone early to bed; the rain prevented evening callers from returning home unless they had coats or umbrellas. By midnight, however, even the unprotected could go out again. The storm had ceased. But like many such storms, it disappointed all who hoped for a change in temperature. Friday, July 29th dawned with the sun shining once more, and once more the weather was sultry.

The light streaming into the upper rooms of the Fifth Avenue Hotel, about half past five, wakened one of the guests who had a room on the Twenty-third Street side. This was Major-General Francis P. Blair, a veteran of the Mexican and the Civil Wars. He had commanded a division at Vicksburg, and the 17th Corps during Sherman's campaigns, including the march to the sea. In 1868, having left the Republican for the Democratic party, the latter nominated him for the Vice-Presidency of the United States. The ticket, however, headed by Horatio Seymour, had the misfortune to contest the election with General Grant, so that Francis P. Blair soon belonged to that class of the peculiarly obscure who have run for the office of Vice-President. He comes early into this story, and he goes out of it soon, but it is rare for an ex-candidate for the second post in the Government to be a witness in a murder case, so I have chosen to let you see the events of the first few moments of the day through the eyes of the Major-General. When he rose from bed, and went to the window to draw the shutters, he stood for a moment to get what little air he might. The sultriness was already unpleasant. He looked idly across Twenty-third Street, and through a third storey window of the house opposite he beheld a gentleman, clad—as the General himself doubtless was, also—in the innocent night-gown of the period. This was soon to become what Mrs. Wharton calls the Age of Innocence in New York, and of the sinful notions, conceived of foreign powers, pyjamas had not yet gained any large number of adherents in the United States. General Blair noticed that this gentleman, as like a tall garden-lily as the heroine of "Love in the Valley"—pure from the night and splendid for the day—was apparently about to dress. He sat on the side of the bed, he yawned delicately, he seemed to be drawing socks upon his feet. He had black side-whiskers, like Mr. Jasper, and his face was so clearly seen that he was easily identified by the General at a later date. There was nothing in the sight to keep anyone from his bed; noticing that the front door of the gentleman's house seemed to be open at an angle of about 45°, the General closed or partly closed the window shutters, and once more laid himself down to sleep.

Thirty minutes later wild shouts and halloos, cries for

help, floated up from the street to General Blair's room. He went again to the window, parted the shutters, and looked out. On the steps of the house opposite stood two men; one of the black whiskers, still incompletely clad, and another, younger and slighter, also in night clothes. Both men were wildly excited, shouting and crying pitifully, and toward them was running up the street, a police officer, while from across the street came a man in workman's clothes. This time the General noticed something about the black whiskered man which he was perfectly sure was not true when he had seen him before; the breast of his night-gown was stained with blood, and he seemed to be wearing red slippers. Another glance showed this also was due to blood; his socks were soaked in it. The cries of the men were still so incoherent, their actions so confused that General Blair was unable to make out whether he was witnessing the result of a fight, or of an accident. He rang his bell and when a servant came, sent him downstairs to ask the cause of the trouble. There was a long delay, but finally the man came back, out of breath, and in a state of wild excitement. The news which he brought was that murder had been done in that peaceful looking house across the street; and that the owner of it, old Mr. Nathan, was lying dead in his room, with his head beaten almost out of recognition.

Now, whether the name of Benjamin Nathan meant much or not to General Blair (who lived—I mean it literally—in Missouri) it meant much to New York, where the story of the death took the place on the front pages of the newspapers which the Franco-Prussian war had been occupying. It was reported and commented upon all over the world,—even in Russia, where the Jewish publications discussed the tragedy which had befallen an eminent and highly respected Jew. It caused the New York Stock Exchange to order its flag at half-mast for the death of its fellow-member, and to offer a reward of $10,000 for the discovery of his murderer. It shocked the religious organizations, the charitable societies, and the business firms with which Mr. Nathan was associated, where he was regarded as a man at once devout, kindly, and honorable. It filled Twenty-third Street for days with crowds of people, who came to gaze at the windows on the second floor. Stages either drove slowly past the house, or stopped altogether to give the passengers a chance to stare at the place. Private carriages, in a long procession, went slowly through the street all day, their occupants leaning out to catch a glimpse of the scene.

Benjamin Nathan, the son of a widely known and highly respected family, was born in New York in 1813, and was therefore about fifty-seven years old. He was a man of medium figure, if not small in stature, wearing white side whiskers, and spectacles, without which his sight was extremely defective. His expression was agreeable and benevolent; he was not known to have any enemies. His fortune was large; he was ranked as one of the wealthy men of the community. He was a good citizen, charitable in his acts and inclinations. His family consisted of a wife and eight children, four sons and four daughters. The sons were named Harmon, Frederick, Washington, and Julian, and all of the family, apparently, with exception of Mr. Nathan himself, and two of the sons, Frederick and Washington, were, on the night of the murder, at their summer home in Morristown, New Jersey. These three had slept in the Twenty-third Street house, as well as the housekeeper, Mrs. Kelly, and her son, William, a man of twenty-five, who acted as chore-boy, messenger, and general helper. Mr. Nathan had come into town on business on Thursday the 28th, and his decision to stay over night was—according to one account—a surprise to the housekeeper. The house was in the hands of upholsterers and decorators. She had prepared him a temporary bed, with a heap of mattresses, in the room on the second floor. He had been with Frederick and Washington early in the evening until they left him, separately, not to return to the house until after midnight. They came in, Frederick the earlier, and assured themselves of their father's presence as they passed his room on their way to the floor above. In the morning, both rose early, as the father and the two sons planned to go to the synagogue to offer prayers in commemoration of some near relative, the anniversary of whose death fell on July 29th. This was an annual custom of the family. Washington Nathan, coming down stairs, still in his night clothes, had discovered his father's dead body, had shouted and alarmed his brother, and the two had rushed into the street, calling loudly for help. Their cries had been heard by General Blair, who had thus witnessed the opening scenes of the tragedy. It was in the moment when Frederick Nathan, before he rushed outdoors, knelt beside his father's body to see if he were indeed dead, that his night-shirt was stained, and his white socks, as he stepped into the pool of blood which surrounded the murdered man, assumed their dreadful color.

The policeman on the beat came running to the house, and a porter from the Fifth Avenue Hotel followed shortly after. The two sons and the police officer went up again to the second storey and entered the room which had served Mr. Nathan as a temporary bed-chamber. The body, clad only in a night-gown, lay on the floor in the doorway between this room and a small adjoining room which was used as a study and office. There were clear indications of a ferocious attack and a violent struggle. The wounds were of the most shocking description; the floor, walls and frame of the door were stained with blood. A chair was over-turned, a small safe in the study was standing open, and on the heap of mattresses was an empty cash-box. During the search of the house, Frederick Nathan observed on the floor, and pointed out to the officer, an iron bar, stained with blood. It was a carpenter's "dog,"—a strange weapon, but evidently that with which the crime had been committed.

Such, in brief, were the facts which came to light on the first day, and were recorded in the newspapers. *The Evening Post* printed an editorial article on "The Season of Murders,"—there was, according to more than one paper, what we call a "crime wave." A proclamation by Mayor Hall specified the rewards, which soon came to be offered; altogether, with those named by the City, and by the Nathan family, they amounted to $47,000, of which $30,000 were for the discovery of the murderer, and the remainder, in varying sums, for different articles of property which were stolen, or thought to be stolen, from the house, and for the identification of the "dog." The articles were three diamond studs, two watches, and a gold medal.

As early as Sunday, July 31st, and probably before that, the city was buzzing with rumors of suspicion. For the most part these were directed toward Washington Nathan. Few, if any, well informed persons credited them, but all had to admit their existence. Mr. James L. Ford, who has not only written on the Nathan murder, but who is in possession of much authoritative information on the subject, believes that the rumors which sought to connect Washington Nathan with his father's death originated wholly with a spiteful reporter for a sensational newspaper. According to Mr. Ford's information, the reporter called at the Nathan house while the family were bewailing their loss in the devout fashion demanded by their ancient orthodox custom. Trying to intrude at this moment, he was unceremoniously turned from the door. Out of revenge, he wrote an article pointing at Washington Nathan.[1] This article appeared Sunday, July 31st, and on the same day the *Herald* published an editorial article in which suspicion was strongly directed toward "the inmates of the house," while the police were advised to begin their examinations within and not outside Mr. Nathan's home.

The grounds for direct suspicion of Washington Nathan were slight. It was true that he had been the

[1] *The Sun* makes this charge against the reporter with circumstantial detail. The newspaper which printed the article in question was *The Sunday Mercury*.

last person known to see his father alive, and the first to discover the dead body. He was somewhat dissipated in his habits, and had been reproved by his father for this reason. The charge was made—for no apparent cause—that he was in dire need of money. It soon appeared that during the evening of July 28th he had been in company which could not even be called doubtful. Those who hold that irregularity in personal morals is next door to crime of any description, no matter how infamous nor how violent, found this good enough cause to make them believe the worst. And there was the difficulty of deciding how a murderer from outside had entered the house. No other way could be discovered than the front door, by which he seemed to have departed.

Against all this could be urged that Washington Nathan's demeanor from the first, was of a kind which speedily convinced nearly all the investigators of his innocence. The differences between him and his father were shown to be slight, and to have been hardly more than those which existed in the case of Frederick or may naturally arise in almost any family. And finally, as Mr. Ford says, the suspicions pointing toward Washington Nathan were "unbelievable," on account of the veneration felt toward parents by Jews of the high caste of this family. Parricide is a crime practically unknown among them.

Newspaper stories, speculations, rumors, and suspicions were New York's only fare until early in the following week when the coroner's inquest opened at the Seventh District Judicial Court, Twenty-second Street and Seventh Avenue. Something definite could then be expected. Both Frederick and Washington Nathan were present. They are described as having olive complexions and curly black hair; Frederick wore black side-whiskers and moustache, Washington only a slight black moustache. Frederick's age, by one account, was twenty-six, and his brother's was twenty-four. Another statement makes Washington only twenty-two. He is further described as five feet, ten inches, in height, slender, and "of a nervous temperament." Both looked guiltless and at ease.

The officer on the beat, John Mangam, was examined. He testified that he was about one hundred feet from the house when he saw the two brothers on the steps in their night-gowns. In response to their calls for help he ran to them, entered the house, went upstairs and viewed the body. He thought that it was still warm, although a few minutes later, after sending to the hotel for a doctor, he felt of the body again and found it cold. He testified that it was Frederick and not Washington who had the blood on his night-clothes. It was Frederick, said the policeman, who pointed out the "dog." Mangam further said that he had tried the front door of the Nathan house at 1.30 and at 4.30 A. M. and had found it locked. He declared that it was his custom to try every door on his beat two or three times in the course of the night. This statement seems to have been accepted by the coroner and the jury, although a correspondent in *The World* said that it was flagrant nonsense, that he had often watched policemen passing up and down the street on their beats at night, and that it was never their custom to trouble themselves at all with the doors.

Dr. Joseph E. Janvrin, the physician for the Fifth Avenue Hotel, testified that he had arrived at the house soon after 6.05 A. M. Mr. Nathan had been dead, in his opinion, three or four hours, or a little longer. The "dog" had caused the wounds. One murderer could have done the deed alone, and it might have happened as early as one or two o'clock. He did not believe that there had been any struggle. (This belief was later contradicted by another medical witness, Dr. Anthony Ruppener, and the coroner's physician, Dr. Beach.)

General Blair was called, and gave testimony which has already been described. The importance of it lay chiefly in his positive identification of Frederick Nathan as the man he saw first, and without blood-stains on his night-gown. When he saw him the second time, outside the house, the blood-stains were there, and thus Frederick's account of their origin was corroborated.

Walton H. Peckham, whose house stood at the south-west corner of Twenty-third Street and Fifth Avenue, appeared next. His was the nearest house to the east from the Nathan home, but there was a space of eighty (?) feet between them. He and his wife heard sounds during the night which they believed to come from their neighbor's house. At first, Mrs. Peckham thought that there was a burglar in her own home, but it soon became apparent that the noise was outside. According to the immemorial custom of wives, she requested her husband to get up and investigate, and in the equally invariable manner of husbands, he declined. After they had been awakened by the first sounds they lay awake and listened. Then they heard a loud noise, as if someone were shutting a door violently, after that there were three distinct sounds, the first of which was dull and heavy. At last they both arose and Mrs. Peckham went into an adjoining room, leaned out of the window, and listened. This, Mr. Peckham was sure, happened between 2 and 2.30 A. M. although he did not look at his watch. He fixed the time because they had already had "a good sound sleep,"—not a very convincing method of calculation. As the storm had been severe, it occurred to them that perhaps the Nathan house had been struck by lightning. Evidently, however, as they did not see it actually burst into flames, they went back to bed. Like Donalbain and his room-mate, when murder stalked abroad in Macbeth's castle, they did say their prayers and addressed them again to sleep.

In comment upon Mr. Peckham's testimony, it seems strange that on a night when windows must everywhere have been open, more people did not hear the noise created by the attack upon Mr. Nathan. A chair was overturned, other furniture was disarranged, and about ten blows were struck with an iron bar upon a human skull. The storm was over by midnight, and the murder did not take place until the rain and thunder had ceased. Or had all windows in the neighborhood been closed during the storm, and were the sleepers around about reposing in stuffy bed-rooms after the tempest had passed? The Major-General's window would seem to have been open, at any rate, and yet he, directly across the street, does not mention having heard anything until the daylight awakened him. The Peckhams, somehow, do not sound like folk who would have been exigent upon the subject of fresh air, and yet they did hear the noises. It can only be explained by the commonplace remark that some persons are light sleepers. One inmate of the Nathan house, Mrs. Kelly, as will appear, did think that she heard "something." For the other people in the house, the unsatisfactory explanation must be that the walls were thick, the house was well built and sound-proof. It is said that Mr. Nathan, within two weeks of his death, had been heard to congratulate himself that he had a comfortable, strongly-built house, in a neighborhood where he was secure from molestation.

James Nies, a newsboy, thirteen years old, testified that he was delivering newspapers on Twenty-third Street, shortly after 5 o'clock that morning. He saw a man "dressed like a mason," pick up on the steps of the Nathan house a yellow piece of paper which looked "like a check," and walk away with it. James professed to be familiar with the appearance of checks. This scrap of paper proved to be one of the innumerable clews which might mean something or nothing, but only served to confuse the police and the detectives. Was it indeed a check, or an important "document" (dear to the hearts of the writers of melodrama) which had been dropped by the murderer in his flight? And had he, or some "confederate" disguised as a "mason" returned, in the manner of romance, to recover the precious slip? (Why did he adopt that particular disguise?) Or was it a stray bit of paper, perhaps merely a handbill, which the thrifty mason thought might be worth examining, since it was lying in front of a rich man's house?

Whatever the truth, neither mason nor yellow scrap of paper came forward in answer to advertisements.

There was no lack of investigation of clews, no lack of rewards offered, no lack of amateur assistance for the officers, nor of newspaper communications from "Judex," "Pro Bono Publico," and their clan. No point was too minute to wrangle about. Chief Jourdan of the police received five hundred letters within a few days. The murderer, with his customary ubiquity, was being arrested two or three times a day. By the time James Nies had given his testimony and excited the envy of every newsboy in New York, the inquest had been in progress for two or three days, for I have greatly compressed the columns of stenographic reports of questions and answers printed by the papers. About August 8th extras were on the streets; the murderer had been arrested, this time in Nyack. A detective had indeed rushed up to that town, in response to a rumor, but all he found was that someone had been told by someone that another person had seen a man "who looked as if" —etc.

At about the same time, a letter signed "A. K. H.", came from Washington, offering to return "the papers" if $800 should be left inside the railing of Grace Church, at a designated place, on August 9th, at eight o'clock in the evening. As the letter did not arrive until after that hour, the police decided, for that and for other reasons, that A. K. H. was but a comedian. Among the oddest incidents of the week was the unpleasant predicament which Mr. Thomas Dunphy got himself into. Mr. Dunphy was a lawyer, once a partner of Edwin

James, the disbarred English barrister. He was calling on some ladies in Brooklyn, and undertook to amuse them with an account of his theory of the Nathan murder. Like his former partner, he had a taste for dramatics, and so put his narrative into the first person singular. Delicious thrills ran up and down the spines of the listeners, as Mr. Dunphy, standing in the middle of the room, brandishing an air-drawn weapon, recited his yarn. He showed Mr. Nathan little or no mercy. "The old man was advancing upon me! With a single bound I sprang toward him! Bringing down my weapon with one powerful blow, I stretched him at my feet!" And so on.

Unluckily, there was a young lady who had not been admitted to the room, but was listening at the key-hole. She became convinced that the red-handed criminal was indeed within, and when she ran out of the house, and called a policeman, her agitation was genuine and convincing. The officer, not at all averse to $30,000 reward and undying glory, rushed inside, collared Mr. Dunphy and dragged him off to the police station. Here, the captain was doubtful but wary. He did not know the lawyer, nor altogether believe his avowals of innocence, and offers of identification, but he allowed the officer to take him over to New York for Chief Jourdan's inspection. In New York, Mr. Dunphy was recognized and exonerated, but his discharge, like his arrest, had to take place in Brooklyn. After some delay he was carried back—thus spending a weary night, part of it in a dungeon cell, and part on the Brooklyn ferries. He was at last released,—doubtless a convert to the belief that for a safe literary style the use of the third personal pronoun is unsurpassed.[2]

After the foregoing paragraph was written, my sympathy with Mr. Dunphy in his sufferings was still further aroused by the discovery that he was a fellow-author, and of a book about murders! In a book-shop some thousands of miles from the place where this was written, I came upon "Remarkable Trials of All Countries . . ." by "Thomas Dunphy of the New York Bar, and Thomas J. Cummings of the New York Press." It is almost wholly devoted to murder trials. My copy is dated, New York, 1870, but the book was first published three years earlier. Mr. Dunphy's indiscretion in Brooklyn is the more remarkable to me in that he had not learned, by the time of the Nathan murder, that it is well for writers on this subject to walk carefully, since they are under constant suspicion of dabbling in a little murder on their own account, merely to gain knowledge and experience.

When the inquest was resumed—at a court down town—Patrick M'Guvin, (or Govern) a porter at the Fifth Avenue Hotel, told how he had been called from his work of washing off the side-walk with a hose, had

[2] Since the day when the butterfly, to impress his wife, threatened to destroy Solomon's temple with one blow of his foot, the desire to shine before "the women folks" has led many a male person into difficulties. A taxi-driver, a year after the Rosenthal murder in New York, sought to give some young lady passengers, to whom he was showing the sights, the worth of their money by driving to the scene of the crime, and telling how he "saw it all" the night it happened. The young ladies were conscientious citizens; they noted his number and flew to the police. The taxi-driver had an unpleasant hour, explaining to the authorities that he was simply an unmitigated liar, that he "was lying all through, and could prove it, too," and that he was really at home sick on that night.

crossed to the Nathan house, and had seen Frederick Nathan direct Mangam's attention to the "dog." He further corroborated the testimony as to the blood-stains on Frederick's night-clothes.

Julius J. Lyons, a nephew of the dead man, stood up to be sworn as a witness, when the proceedings were interrupted by an incident which also helps to explain why life in New York was peculiarly interesting fifty years ago. The Count Joannes arose, and announcing himself as "Chairman of the Nathan Vigilance Committee," objected to the form of oath.

"This man, Sir," said the Count, addressing the Coroner, and indicating the witness, "belongs to the Holy House of Israel. He cannot be sworn in that way." (He referred to the Cross on the cover of the Bible.) "He must have his hat on his head, his face to the east, and his hand on the five books of the Pentateuch."

Mr. Lyons then raised his right hand, and was sworn. Whereupon the Count arose once more. "I protest here!" said he. Coroner Rollins, a little testily, inquired: "For whom do you appear?" The Count courteously replied: "I appear as an *amicus curiae*. I protest that the witness cannot be sworn except in the manner I have stated." Mr. Lyons was then asked by a juror if the oath he had taken would bind his conscience as much as any other. He said that it would; the Count subsided, and the witness was examined. As so frequently happens, the testimony which was only procured after this struggle, ironically proved to be unimportant, except that it included a statement that the relations between Washington Nathan and his father were loving.

THE LATE BENJAMIN NATHAN.—FROM A PHOTOGRAPH BY BRADY.

*From "Leslie's Weekly"*

Benjamin Nathan

*From "Leslie's Weekly"*

Harmon Nathan — Washington Nathan — E. B. Hart — Frederick Nathan

The Nathan Inquest

The Count Joannes, who thus flashed into prominence for three minutes, was a man of English birth. Instead of being, like Edwin James, a lawyer turned actor, he was an actor who had been called to the bar. Player, dramatist, historian, and theatrical manager, he had enacted *Richmond* to the *Richard* of Junius Brutus Booth, and seems to have been the victim of Booth's celebrated attack upon his stage antagonist on that occasion when the famous actor tried, with too great realism, to put an end to *Richmond* forever. The Count had been known, before 1833, as George Jones, but in that year "he was installed as Count of Sertorii of the Holy Roman Empire of the First Commander of the Imperial Order of Golden Knight and Count Palatine." Unless this ceremony was one which might be performed by mail, it must have taken place during one of Mr. Jones's visits to Europe, for it does not sound like a thing which could be done in New York. Afterwards, he was never seen in public without his insignia of knighthood. He wore the jewel and pendant upon a black scarf, in harmony with the general sombreness of his attire. After an elaborate public examination he had been admitted to practice as an attorney and counsellor-at-law in the courts of New York, but in 1871 he returned to the stage. He appeared in that year as *Richard*, and was applauded by an audience which had come to scoff. He was, at this period at least, an intelligent and dignified actor, but his final years were pathetic. Leading a troupe in Shakespearean repertoire at the Academy of Music and at the Lyceum in the late seventies, he was cruelly and unmercifully ridiculed by the audiences. He died in utter poverty in 1879, a pitiful exit for one whose lectures had been rewarded by a medal from a Shakespearean society, whose history of ancient America had been praised by the great Duke of Wellington, who had been presented at various European courts, and mingled enough with fashionable folk to have his portrait drawn by Count D'Orsay.

With the appearance of Mrs. Anne Kelly, Mr. Nathan's housekeeper, the list of witnesses at last reached the persons who had actually been in the house on the night of the murder. After an unsuccessful attempt to keep from telling about an unhappy event of her early life, Mrs. Kelly was allowed to proceed to matters of relevance, and these were, briefly, that she had last seen Mr. Nathan alive at about 10 P. M., when she had carried some iced-water to his room. She fastened the doors front and rear, and all the windows. She was awakened by the storm, and heard nothing thereafter until awakened in the morning by the cries of the two sons. Mrs. Kelly was accused by one newspaper of changing her testimony, in regard to another noise in the night. One report does represent her as saying that she heard nothing but the sound of the storm, while another newspaper records her statement that she thought she heard another sound, but could not tell what it was, and did not get up to investigate, nor stay awake to listen.

Washington Nathan was, of course, the witness for whom reporters and newspaper readers were waiting. He described himself as a commission merchant at 25 Water Street. In the early evening, July 28th, he had been with his father at the synagogue. Later, he left the older man at an aunt's house, and commenced an hour or two of aimless wandering.

He walked up Fifth Avenue to the St. James Hotel, he strolled over to Twenty-fourth Street and Broadway, then into Madison Square, where, for a time, he listened to a band which was playing in the park. Meeting a friend, he went with him again to the St. James, where each had a glass of sherry. He walked down Broadway to Fifth Avenue, where he met "these two girls,"—indicating two young persons, (as Pooh Bah would say) who were apparently in Court. With them he wandered over to Delmonico's, where he said *au revoir*, and went into the coffee-room to idle about and look at the pictorial papers until half-past eight. The St. James then attracted him again for a while (there is no reference to sherry), then he wandered back to the Fifth Avenue Hotel, into which he went and held conversation with a Mr. Joel Wolfe. About 9 he left the Hotel, "got into a green car, one of the Thirty-fourth Street, cross-town cars" and in it went down to East Fourteenth Street, near the Academy of Music. Into a house there, number 104, he went, and there he stayed until about midnight. At that hour, he was detained a little by the rain, but at last he could venture out, and when he did so he went up Broadway to Twenty-first Street, entered Brown and Kingsley's and had a Welsh rabbit. Arrived at home, he knew by a system which he and his brothers had with the key, that he was the last to return. He put out the light in the hall, paused a second or two at the door of his father's room and saw that he was asleep, went up to his own room on the third floor, and so to bed. He was undisturbed during the rest of the night, woke of himself a little before six, was thirsty and started downstairs for some water. Met his brother with whom he exchanged a word or two, and continued down the stairs, intending to rouse his father, for the religious ceremony, as well as to get the water aforesaid. As he descended he noticed that the front door was open, but thought nothing of it, as he supposed Mrs. Kelly was up and at work. The light in his father's room was dim, except for a ray of sunlight which streamed in through a chink in the shutter. Once in the room, and looking about, he discovered the body on the floor, and instantly shouted to his brother. As soon as they had assured themselves of the tragedy they rushed outside to call for help.

Questioned at great length about his relations with his father, he denied any serious quarrels, but admitted having been reproved for his "habits." His father had furnished him with $5,000 as his capital in business. He had no fixed allowance, but his father gave him money when he required it. He had never spent more than $3,000 a year; there was no foundation for the report that he had spent $30,000 in one year. As far as can be gathered from the reports, he gave an impression of perfect candor.

It was felt necessary to corroborate his statements as to the hours between nine and twelve, so the name was called of "Clara Dale," and, as a novelist would say: there was a flutter in the Court. For a description of a young lady like the one who went under this romantic *nom de guerre*, it is customary to borrow a brief phrase from Mr. Kipling, about "the oldest profession in the world"; or else to fall back upon the proverbs of Solomon, the son of David, King of Israel. The reporters of the New York papers did neither; as yet they knew not Mr. Kipling, and they forgot Solomon; they looked upon her, and lo, she was very fair. The man from the *Herald* remarked that she "was very gaily attired in a costly dress of green striped silk, embellished with all the usual paraphernalia of panier, flounces and trimmings. She wore light colored lavender kid gloves and over a jaunty round hat of the latest pattern was spread a green veil which hung down over her face almost completely hiding it from view. Beneath this she wore a black lace 'masked battery' which totally covered the upper portion of her face." *The World* reporter, totally neglecting the ancient truth that this was one whose feet go down to death and her steps take hold on hell, dwelt upon her hair in "waterfall and puffs," her gaiters in the latest style, "with the preposterous high brass heels, and white pearl buttons and tassels. Her face was full and fair, with large blue eyes, and her physique and carriage were stately." Only *The Evening Post*, faithful guardian of New York's virtue, ignored Miss Dale's green and white dress, her waterfalls and puffs, and everything about her except the briefest and most austere report of her testimony. For the readers of that paper, she barely existed. Her testimony *was* extremely brief, and to the effect that she met Washington Nathan, as described, about 7.30, that she parted from him on the street, met him again at 9 and was in his company until about 12.10. *The World*, in its devotion to democracy and the cause of the people, recorded the conversation of two sturdy citizens who stood in Court and made sarcastic remarks about the deference paid to the beautiful Miss Dale by the assistant district attorney, as compared with his treatment of the honest working-woman, Mrs. Kelly. But that, said one of these rough diamonds, was due to the fact that Clara Dale "lives in Fourteenth Street." There seems to have been a suggestion of the high world of fashion in the words "Fourteenth Street" which quite escapes us to-day.

William Kelly, son of the housekeeper, general runner of errands and handy-man at 12 West Twenty-third Street. A nervous, rather sickly looking man, and a veteran of the late war. He had been in this country since 1860, coming hither from Ireland. In 1864 he enlisted in the United States Army at Lawrence, Massachusetts, going there from New York for the purpose. Why had he done so? Apparently because Massachusetts was paying at that time a bounty of $500 for enlistments. He had given three fifths of the sum to his mother, and had served in the Army until his discharge in July, 1865. Either wounded or sick as a result of this experience, he was receiving a pension of $8.00 a month from the Government. He lived on this, and on an occasional tip for doing errands; apparently allowed food and lodging in return for blacking boots and other services. He was thoroughly brow-beaten by the assistant district attorney; he had the misfortune to be the son of parents who were not married, and his attempts to conceal this fact seemed to anger the examiner. He had heard nothing during the night, had come down stairs in the morning and heard the sons shouting that their father was killed. There seems to have been reason for believing that some of his associates and friends were dwellers upon the edge of the criminal world, and he was inferentially accused of bounty-jumping, desertion, drunkenness, burglary, conspiracy, loafing, fraud, sneak-thievery, and consorting with dissolute and rascally persons.

A large part of one day was devoted to the examination of a number of shipwrights and carpenters as to the nature of the "dog." This was one of the strangest and most inexplicable weapons which ever figured in a celebrated murder. There it was, and plainly enough it was the weapon of the assassin, but exactly what was it, and where had it come from? Did its presence indicate that the murderer came from outside the house or not? And if it showed that he came from without, did it prove that he was an expert cracksman, or a clumsy thief? Folk wrangled upon these questions, wrote letters to the papers about the "dog," and arrived with absolute assurance at exactly opposite conclusions. It was a bar of iron about eighteen inches long, turned down and sharpened at each end, somewhat in the shape of a staple. Its picture was printed in *Leslie's Weekly*. Leonard H. Boole, a shipwright, testified that such an implement would be used to lay the flooring in yachts and small vessels, but he added that he had never seen a "dog" so small as this. A plumber who had worked in the house said that he had never seen a "dog" there; other laborers agreed with him; a mason had seen one in the stable, but it was not like this one.

Frederick Nathan testified, after having been administered "the special oath," probably to the intense pleasure of Count Joannes. After parting from his father on Thursday evening he made a call in Brooklyn at the house of some friends. He reached home a little after midnight, and as he went upstairs exchanged a few words with the elder Nathan on the pertinent subject of iced-water. (The testimony of both sons indicates that the door of Mr. Nathan's room stood open; that would be expected on such a warm night, but the point is significant, bearing upon the sounds that the struggle and the blows would have made, and the fact that they were not heard by anybody in the house.) He was undisturbed during the night, and when he woke went to the window to observe the weather. He had begun to dress, under the eye of General Blair, but must have been proceeding slowly, for he was only partly dressed when his brother called out from below. He ran down stairs, saw his father lying on the floor, and knelt beside him to see if he were dead. He thought the body must have been cold at that time, as he felt the chill as he stepped in the pool of blood. He denied any disagreement with his father about money, and said that neither he, nor, in his belief, his brother, knew the provisions of his father's will. He was asked many questions about William Kelly, his past conduct, and his demeanor when he heard of the murder. Kelly was carrying a pair of boots in his hand at the moment, and the question whether or not he dropped them was much discussed, as some of the disputants thought that the fact of his holding fast to the boots indicated his lack of surprise about the news, and hence a guilty knowledge.

The final witness was Dr. John Beach, the coroner's physician. He made an examination of the room, and of the body, at 2 P. M. on July 29th. Some of the fingers of the right hand were broken, there were wounds on various parts of the body, three on the forehead and six, at least, on the back of the head. The wound on the forehead was frightful. He believed that the body had been moved after death, and that the "dog" could have inflicted every wound. As he reconstructed the scene, Mr. Nathan entered the room bent forward and peering to discover the cause of the noise he had heard. (The man working at the safe?) The murderer heard him and waited till he crossed the threshold, in order to give him a stunning blow from behind. This brought the old gentleman to his knees; he tried to crawl out of the room while blows were rained on the back of his head. Mr. Nathan mechanically put up his hands to protect himself, and had his fingers broken by the iron bar. Finally he lay on the floor, with his face slightly turned, when his assailant struck him the final terrible blow on the forehead. The murderer then dragged the corpse along the floor, as bloodstains indicated, and turned it over on its back. Only one man was engaged in the crime and he left the house with blood on his clothing.

The inquest closed on August 12, the jury finding no verdict.

One of the numerous and confusing stories, current even before the inquest, was told by Patrick Devoy, caretaker of a house in West Twenty-second Street. This was the home of Professor S. F. B. Morse, inventor of the telegraph, at 5 West Twenty-second Street. The

Nathan stables were next to the Morse house, and Devoy returning at 12.30 A. M. on July 29th, found a coach and pair standing in front of the stables. A man was lying in the coach, and he was requested by Devoy to move on. Devoy believed that he whispered to somebody else in the coach, but he did not move away. Going inside the house, the caretaker found that his wife had seen the carriage arrive at 10.30 P. M., and she had observed it to stand there throughout the storm. At 1.30 a man mounted the box, and the coach was driven away,—"rapidly," of course.

In the days and months following the inquest there were a number of "confessions" and accusations. A man named Hayes, and another called Robert Kipling, are said to have been arrested at one time or another. A burglar, named John T. Irving, who was under arrest in California, made a "confession" implicating others, in order to get a free passage to New York. He was brought East, but failed to convince anybody, and vanished into prison. George Ellis, a convict in prison at Sing Sing, declared that if he were in New York he could establish the identity of the murderer of Mr. Nathan. He was brought down with great secrecy, and given, as a first test, a chance to identify the "dog." Chief Jourdan sent to hardware shops and procured about twenty-five "dogs" of different sizes and shapes. These he smeared with blood and threw all on the table where lay the real weapon. Ellis came into the room and "without an instant's hesitation picked out the one with which Mr. Nathan had been killed." Then he said that some time before his commitment to Sing Sing, he and a burglar named Forrester had planned to rob the Nathan house. Murder was no part of their scheme, for they had intended to enter in the summer, during the absence of the family; and it was a mere accident, he said, which led his pal to select a night on which the old gentleman happened to be at home. His theory was that Forrester, finding himself surprised and fearful of an alarm, killed Mr. Nathan. He knew the "dog," because it was one with which they had often worked before.

An attempt was made to find Forrester, and on March 9, 1871, *The New York Times* announced "a full confession" from "the Nathan murderer," Billy Forrester. Editorially, the paper expressed a belief that the right man had been caught at last. A month later it printed a description of him from the *Avalanche* of Memphis, Tennessee. Born in Scotland in 1835 he had come to New York, where in 1865 he was shanghaied on a ship for California. He finally drifted into crime, and became a notorious cracksman, being sentenced to a term of years in the prison at Joliet, Illinois. Nevertheless, New York did not get him; on August 3, 1871, the *Times* said that Forrester had escaped to Scotland.

He appears again in the newspapers in September, 1872, when the *Times* changes its belief in his guilt. He had been found in Texas and fetched to New York by a detective named Phil Farley. Forrester was represented by the celebrated firm of Howe and Hummel,[3]

[3] Readers may learn, or refresh their memories, about this firm by consulting in Arthur Train's *True Stories of Crime* the chapter called "The Downfall of a Criminal Lawyer"; or for a treatment of the subject slightly disguised as fiction, the same author's *The Confessions of Artemas Quibble.*

and examined before Judge Dowling in the Court of Special Sessions beginning on September 18, 1872. George Ellis, as a convict who could not testify unless pardoned, was not produced against him. Too many criminals had secured favors by professing to have information about the Nathan case. The identification of Forrester with the murderer rested upon an affidavit dated the same day, and made by Miss Annie Keenan, a music teacher from Fort Lee. Miss Keenan had been walking in West Twenty-third Street at about 8.30 on the evening of July 28, 1870. She had noticed a man with a "crazy look" in his eye, and some rigid implement up his sleeve. He went under the stoop and disappeared into the Nathan house by the basement, and as he did so his arm struck the stone work and the implement gave out a clang like an iron bar,—like a "dog" in fact. All that he failed to do, apparently, was to turn to her and announce: "I am Billy Forrester, about to commit the famous Nathan murder!" Miss Keenan persisted that she recognized Forrester as the man with the crazy look and the iron bar, and denied an assertion that she was near-sighted. She gave a proof of her eyesight in court, but her affidavit was far too good; Miss Keenan has the chief claim to the rôle of sensational female witness, who frequently appears, usually much earlier, about two weeks after a mysterious crime, with a story which fits uncannily into the requirements of the situation, and indicates a careful attention to newspaper reports.

The case against Forrester failed. District Attorney Garvin said that while he was morally satisfied that the prisoner was in the city at the time of the murder, "and was connected with the offence," nevertheless "the technical facts . . . would fail in making out a case." Justice Dowling was merely satisfied "morally" that Forrester was in the *State* at the time, but he realized that the testimony against him would not bear cross-examination. He was therefore constrained to discharge the prisoner. Illinois, however, still desired Billy Forrester. The *Times* reported that he offered to reveal the real murderer in exchange for a pardon from the Governor of Illinois. The offer was not accepted; on September 27th he was on his way back to Joliet to serve the rest of his term.

Mr. Hummel's story is more dramatic and somewhat conflicting. The witness was "a young Catholic girl" on her way to mass, in the early morning. (I do not find her in the newspapers of that day.) She had seen two men come hurriedly down the steps of the Nathan house. At the inquiry in 1872 she confronted Forrester, and the latter showed great agony as she looked searchingly at him for "fully ten minutes." She said she believed him to be the man, but could not be positive. This also was unsatisfactory to the Court and at the end of this ordeal, and after his discharge, Forrester sent for Mr. Hummel and begged to be sent back to Joliet. He went "with absolute relief and contentment." Mr. Hummel said that many times had he been asked to save men from jail, but never, in all his criminal experience, had a man pleaded to be sent to jail. Mr. Hummel closes thus: "In regard to Forrester I cannot speak fully without violating professional honor, for the man was a client of my office; but I can say this, that from what

I learned of him, Washington Nathan had no more to do with the killing of his father than I."

A curious and inconclusive tale came to light about 1899, showing how long the mystery lingered in people's minds. At that time there died in a small town in New Hampshire a woman named Irene McCready. In 1870, in her house on Fourteenth Street had lived Clara Dale. After a long and notorious career in New York, Mrs. McCready had retired to her early home in New Hampshire. After her death, her nieces said that their aunt had told them a story substantially as follows. On the morning after the tragedy a woman who had a similar establishment on Twenty-seventh Street had come to her in great alarm. A beautiful Spanish woman, who lived in the Twenty-seventh Street house, had left it at ten o'clock on that night, and had been absent until three in the morning. She was known to carry a key to the Nathan home. "And," said the woman, "there was murder done in that house last night. What shall I do about it?" Irene McCready's advice was brief, "Keep your mouth shut," said she. "Nobody knows you, and I think 'Wash' Nathan can prove an alibi by Clara Dale."

In Mr. Walling's "Recollections of a New York Chief of Police" (1887) there is a chapter on the Nathan murder, which gives the impression of having been written from a memory not always reliable. The chapter points, at first, to Washington Nathan. He was unfilial in his conduct; he was, on that night, "clinking glasses with the *demi-monde*"; and he wore, for a week after the murder, a handkerchief like a bandage around his neck. The implication of this, of course, is that he was concealing scars or wounds. The handkerchief is not mentioned by the reporters, who saw him in court at the opening of the inquest, within the week, nor did the artist who drew the sketch of him for *Leslie's Weekly* notice it. Anybody at all familiar with the sensational rumors which are always eagerly repeated by the credulous, will not accept the handkerchief story. In fact, a tale of this kind is conventional in murder cases; it always has great popular success. A similar yarn was current during the investigation of the Hall-Mills murder in New Brunswick, N. J., in 1922. After heaping up suspicions against Washington Nathan, Mr. Walling illogically proceeds to a conclusion of a different nature. His own personal belief, he says, is that William Kelly admitted confederates to the house to rob the safe, and that they committed the graver crime. Finally, Mr. Walling makes the fantastic suggestion that the cause of Chief Jourdan's decline in health, and his death, which occurred soon after the murder, were due to the fact that he solved the mystery, and that the full horror of it was too much for him to bear.

There are invariably those who profess to believe that there is never an undiscovered criminal; that the police know the truth always, but for various reasons, cannot always divulge it.[4] But to think that the discovery of the iniquity of William Kelly and his burglar confederates should actually have undermined the constitution of Chief Jourdan—fairly blasted him with its terror—

[4] As in the Elwell murder in New York, and the Hall-Mills case in New Brunswick, in both of which it is gravely asserted that the police know the murderer's name.

indicates an odd naïveté on the part of Mr. Walling, himself a grizzled ex-chief of police. Officer Mangam is the hero of the Nathan case in the Walling chapter, although that policeman seems nearly to have swooned with excitement at the inquest. Mr. Walling's book is interesting, but its style suggests that it was written, from the Chief's verbal accounts, by some author who had in mind a rural audience, fond of romantic notions and pious jeremiads against all forms of metropolitan wickedness.

The suspicion of guilt, which surrounded Washington Nathan for so long, seemed to have the not surprising effect of still further undermining a character which was probably never strong. He received bequests of $75,000 from his father, $25,000 from his grandmother, and $10,000 from an aunt. His habits and associations continued evil, and he saved nothing from all this. At the death of his mother, in 1879 (she left $1,000,000.) a trust fund of $100,000 was established for him; the income was $5,200. He is remembered as a frequent diner at Delmonico's in the late seventies or early eighties; although his companion would be gay in appearance, he seemed morose and sombre. In 1879 he again achieved unpleasant notoriety: while calling, in the parlor of the Coleman House, upon an actress, a Miss Alice Harrison, he was shot and wounded in the neck by a woman named Fanny Barrett. The bullet lodged in the muscles of the jaw and was never removed. Chief Walling tells of a plan suggested at this time, by a physician, in the event that an operation should be necessary. It was the doctor's intention, while the patient was talkative under the effects of the anæsthetic, to interrogate him about the murder and to settle, once and for all, the problem of his guilt or innocence. The operation not being performed, this scheme failed.

In 1884, having married a Mrs. Arnott, widowed daughter of Colonel J. H. Mapleson, Washington Nathan left America. He lived in a suburb of London and in Paris, where he frequented the Chatham Hotel, alone and unattended, and with a desolate expression of countenance. In 1891, creditors brought suit against him for $1,590, and tried to levy on the income from the trust fund established by his mother's will. The courts, however, decided that this income could not be touched. He was reported in poor health as early as 1887, and on the 25th of July, 1892, died at Boulogne. His hair had turned entirely white in his exile. He was forty-four years old.[5]

Number 12 West Twenty-third Street was naturally full of unhappy associations for the Nathan family. They moved farther up Fifth Avenue. The house was favored by nobody as a dwelling place, and has long been used for business purposes. It is part of a row of shops and stores. Altered nearly out of recognition, it keeps in the interior few traces of its origin as a dwelling-house. The stoop is gone, the windows have been enlarged, and the staircase, down which the brothers ran upon that sultry July morning, has quite vanished.

As there was never any formal trial, the Nathan case remains, except for the testimony at the inquest, one

[5] *New York Times*, July 27, 1892.

which must be studied in the uncertain light of conflicting newspaper reports, rumors, suspicions, and recollections which are based upon a mixture of all these. Washington Nathan had the *opportunity* to commit the crime; Clara Dale's testimony did not establish an alibi for him, as the murder certainly took place after he came home. Her appearance chiefly lent color to the inquest. He was in the house at the time, but so were his brother and the Kellys. Did he have the motive and the disposition to do it? I do not believe that he had.

Who remain? There is the mysterious, beautiful Spaniard, but the story about her is grotesque. There were other reasons, of course, why she could have been absent from home, and the tale that she possessed a key is apocryphal. If she did have one, it could easily have found its way into other and criminal hands, and the problem of the burglar's entrance is solved. What could have been her motive? Did the crime have the appearance of a murder committed by a woman? That question is answered before it is asked. As for Mrs. Kelly, no serious suspicions seem to have been entertained against her; the most that was suggested was a guilty knowledge of her son's participation, gained either before or after the act. Had it been Frederick Nathan who was "clinking glasses" on that night, instead of Washington, the suspicions might have clustered around him, with equal injustice. But he was calling in Brooklyn, and for a New Yorker to show that he was in Brooklyn is as good as a proof that he was, during that time, without fear or reproach. Nobody ever goes to Brooklyn with malefic intent. Lack of adequate motive and of disposition are as much to be urged in behalf of one brother as another.

What about William Kelly? The questions asked him certainly indicate that there was a reason to believe that he had at least one or two unsavory associates. Chief Walling, on the police force at the time, but not necessarily engaged in this investigation, selects Kelly as the man who opened the door to the murderer. But why should he have done this when all three Nathans were there? Had he furnished a key to a back-door, or agreed to unfasten a window each night, and did he then leave it to the burglar's own decision when the entrance was to be made? No one knows; we fish in the dark. I cannot hear Kelly's replies to the questions at the inquest, nor see him as he stood there. But as I read the long columns of fine print in the reports, he seems to me a rather pitiful, but harmless duffer, not up to the part, even, of second murderer.

Out of all the outsiders, out of all that rogues' gallery of cracksmen and burglars, there is seriously to be considered Billy Forrester. George Ellis, himself a convict with favors to seek, charged him with the crime. Abe Hummel's statement is very strong; if you accept that, it amounts to a certainty that Forrester killed Mr. Nathan. *The Times* completely reversed its belief in his guilt. His lawyer, and the District Attorney, however, were in a better position to know. How did he get in? What did he come for? There was, after all, nothing of great value stolen from the house. Was he concealed somewhere in one of the dark rooms when Frederick and Washington entered and went upstairs? Did he wait until he thought Mr. Nathan was asleep before starting to open the safe? Crack a safe with a man asleep in the next room and two more upstairs? Burglars were bold in those days, and they held the police in contempt. How did he dare make the frightful noise which the murder must have occasioned?

Yet somebody dared to do it, and did not instantly hasten away, but stayed at least long enough to assure himself of the fact of death. Again and again there arises the question why the sounds were not heard by others in the house. Chief Byrnes spoke of this as New York's most famous and most mysterious murder. More than thirty years later, and not many hundreds of yards away, in Madison Square Garden, occurred a murder fully as notorious and more scandalous and sensational. But those who hold with DeQuincey that to be readable the story of a murder must contain some element of mystery, will never think that wretched affair comparable in interest with the Nathan case. The Twenty-third Street murder has kept a strange fascination, not because of its scarlet streak, but because it led into so many blind alleys, dark and impossible of exploration.

# "MATE BRAM!"

## "MATE BRAM!"

WHEN a great ship sails from port there can be nothing quiet or inconspicuous about her departure: it is always in the grand manner. If her voyage ends in tragedy, like that of the *Titanic* or the *Lusitania*, it is easy to fancy that she set out with her doom already foreshadowed, as if some hero or king were going out to his last great battle. The little ships slip in and out, beautiful but unnoticed. The most commonplace of them, if it is a sailing-ship and seen at sea may look as graceful as a sea-gull. On board of her, only the landsman, resolutely poetic, can fail to discover that she is usually commanded by a matter of fact person, with an eye to business; and manned by a group whose response to the magic of their surroundings is rather less than that of so many street-car drivers. The sea means to them a rather hard and ill-paid life; but its tediousness affects them less than the better educated and more imaginative man. To him there is the marvel of that blue or gray circle of ocean and sky in whose center he is fixed; the recurring glories of dawn and sunset; and the spell cast by the sea upon the heart of man, which long ago led Tristan to the side of Iseult, and is apt to cause one or two betrothals upon almost every voyage on an ocean-liner.

The names as well as the careers of the little ships

are unknown except to a few people. One of them may run into an adventure which embalms her forever in legal documents; she is quoted in a decision of international law, and her jaunty name enlivens the solemn utterances of judges. Or, like the *Marie Celeste*, she represents an unsolved mystery of the ocean, as much a perpetual topic for the writer of short stories and newspaper articles as the death of the Crown Prince Rudolph.

There used to sail up and down the coasts of the two Americas, or across the Atlantic, a sturdy, commonplace looking ship, called the *Herbert Fuller*. She carried nothing delightful for cargo; neither apes nor peacocks were consigned to her care. On her two most important voyages, at any rate, she was laden with uninteresting lumber. Her life upon the ocean under two names—for she found it advisable to make a change—lasted for twenty-seven years, and so it might be an exaggeration to say that she had an incurable habit for adventure. But from one of her voyages (which began, by the way, upon a Friday) she came into harbor, after only thirteen days at sea, under circumstances grim and terrible indeed, and as the scene of a tragedy which was to perplex two courts and two juries, and even to interest the Supreme Court of the United States. And when she set out on her last, slow voyage, and tried to deliver her last cargo of lumber, she was fated never to arrive, but again the prey of violent men, to go to the bottom of the sea off Monte Carlo, which for a native of Harrington, Maine, like the *Herbert Fuller*, is a long, long way from home.

The *Fuller* was built at Harrington, in 1890; she hailed from Machias. She was a barkentine,—that is, a three masted vessel with the foremast square-rigged, as in a ship, and the other two masts rigged fore-and-aft, like a schooner's. On July 3, 1896, she sailed from Long Wharf, Boston, for Rosario, on the Parana River, Argentine Republic. A few weeks later her name was to stare from the front pages of the newspapers, but her departure interested perhaps only twenty persons. If you search the Marine Record in the *Boston Herald*, for July 4th, 1896, you will find merely this: "Port of Boston: Sailed (yesterday) . . . barkentine *Herbert Fuller*, Rosario; . . ." and below: "The barkentine *Herbert Fuller*, which sailed yesterday for Rosario, anchored in Nantasket Roads (on account of threatening weather)." Later, on July 9, "Sailed from the Roads, brig *Champion* (Br.) Bear River, N. S., sch. *Jacob M. Haskell*, from Red Beach, Me. for Norfolk; barkentine *Herbert Fuller*, Rosario."

There were eleven men and one woman aboard, and a strange assortment they were. Under the microscopic examinations of two murder trials it appeared that two of the men were peculiar if not extraordinary persons, and that the ship was in danger from the moment of departure. She was commanded by a native of Harrington, Captain Charles I. Nash, a man of about forty-two, heavy in frame, with brown hair and a thick brown moustache. He had been a sailor for many years—a captain, it is said, for twenty—and in command of the *Fuller* for five. He owned shares in her amounting to an interest of nearly one third. His wife, Laura, a woman a year or two younger than himself, accompanied her husband upon this voyage according to her custom.

They had been boy and girl together in the same town, had been married for many years and were without children. Captain Nash was a seaman of excellent reputation; he and his wife were apparently devoted to each other, and had often sailed together. Mrs. Nash owned a share or two in the *Fuller;* when they were both aboard, all their fortune was there.

Only one man on the ship had been known to the Captain for any considerable time before sailing. This was the steward, Jonathan Spencer, a mulatto, about twenty-four years old, from the island of St. Vincent, in the British West Indies. He had been at sea for nine or ten years, and had been on one voyage before with Captain Nash on the *Fuller*, to Martinique. The crew were strangers to the Captain, and each other, having shipped only a few days before sailing. In the port watch were Hendrik Perdock, a young Hollander; Francis M. Loheac, a Frenchman who had "left his country without authorization" and, it was alleged, the French Navy without permission; and a rather odd seaman, called "Charley Brown," who had been born forty years before in Sweden. Brown had a habit of talking to himself and making strange gestures.

The starboard watch consisted of Henry J. Slice, a naturalized American citizen, who was by birth a German subject, from Hamburg; Oscar Anderson; and Folke Wassen, both from Sweden.

Occupying rooms which opened from the cabin, or after-house, were the Captain and Mrs. Nash, the two mates, and the passenger. As if the personnel of the ship were arranged for the conventional romance of the sea, the *Fuller* had on board a passenger, a young student from the Lawrence Scientific School of Harvard University. His name was Lester Hawthorne Monks of Brookline, Massachusetts; his age a little over twenty. He had been suffering from a bronchial trouble, and for this reason, and because he was fond of the sea, and had had yachting experiences which he wished to supplement by a long voyage under sail, he once or twice visited the *Fuller*, late in June, and talked with the steward and with the new first mate. He was advised by the mate not to come; for whatever reason it was offered, better advice perhaps, was never given, nor its rejection more earnestly regretted.

Little appears about the second mate. Also new to the *Fuller*, he was a Russian Finn. He was a large man, larger than Captain Nash; his name, August W. Blomberg.

There is a large amount of information on record about the first mate. Called by various combinations of names, he seems to have been entitled to the style of Thomas Mead Chambers Bram. He had been born, as he meticulously explained in court, "on a very small Island, one of the British West India Islands, called St. Kitts." He had, on an official paper, given Nova Scotia as his birthplace, but this apparently was stated in a purely Pickwickian sense. He was thirty-two or three years old, of mixed English and Dutch descent with a strong admixture of negro blood. In appearance, he was a swarthy man, with heavy dark moustache. He ran away from home in 1879 and was shipped as seaman on a schooner from Eastport, Maine, "in the sardine trade."

Afterwards he appeared in New York as a waiter in one of the Dennett restaurants,—a chain of eating places which combined low prices with a strongly religious atmosphere. My recollection of one of them is that directly underneath a wall motto advising you to have faith in Providence, appeared another notice warning you to look out for sneak-thieves, and keep a sharp watch upon your hat and coat.

Young Bram went about the country for a number of years; apparently industrious, and with his emotional nature much influenced by the evangelistic services held in these restaurants. He was "assistant night manager" in one of the New York branches; he came to Boston about 1886 to take charge of a restaurant there; he married, and lived for a time in Cambridge. At different periods he was again in New York; in Chicago, still in Dennett's employment; and once more in New York. Mr. Dennett failed in business, and his former waiter tried to run one of the restaurants for himself, but failed, as his chief had done.

Then he went to sea again, hired by the New York house of G. A. Brett Son and Co. Later, he was mate of the schooner *Henry M. Clark* of Machias; he was captain of a brig from Nova Scotia; and in one capacity or another, on the schooner *China*, when she put into Belize in distress; on the *Cyrus Hall;* the *Nellie Lamper;* on the brig *Highlander* from Philadelphia to Brazilian ports. Returning to New York, his father-in-law secured him the command of a steam lighter. About July, 1895, he went on the barkentine *White Wings* to Brazil. His connection with this ship seems to have ended abruptly.

He served for a time on the steamship *Manning*, and finally arrived in Boston in May, 1896. On June 10 he shipped as first mate on the *Herbert Fuller*, at $40 a month. They loaded her with lumber at Mystic Wharf, and came back to Long Wharf four days before sailing.

The first mate was always interested in religion; he attended sailors' missions, became an exhorter or lay preacher, attending or conducting services in the Dennett restaurants. He had been naturalized as an American citizen in 1888. There were two or three children born of his marriage, but his wife had for some time lived apart from him, in Brooklyn, and he had last seen her about a year before the *Fuller* sailed.

To the state of affairs resulting from the assorted nationalities in the ship's company, and their lack of acquaintance with one another, was added a further complication by the confusion which prevailed about names. The first mate seems at first to have been known to some of those on board as Mr. Brown or Mr. "Brom." This may have been a mere accident of pronunciation, or a misunderstanding, although it was strongly asserted, afterwards, that Mr. Bram did not exactly force a knowledge of his identity and his experiences upon anybody. The sailors did not know him at all by name; to them he was simply "the mate," and they addressed him as "Sir." Probably there was nothing unusual about that. The second mate was known as Mr. Blume or "Blum." Nobody knew the sailors' names; evidently they were called "here you!" and it went at that. Bram referred to Loheac as "Loheez" which perhaps was as near as anybody came to it; and he thought that Slice's name was Harris. Charley Brown was hiding under a bushel the magnificent name of Justus Leopold Westerberg; he had adopted the simpler style, he said, for the convenience of the officers on an English ship in which he had sailed. The explanation sounds reasonable, but when it came out that there had been a bizarre incident in his past, the existence of the *alias* was not allowed to be forgotten. Except for the captain and his wife and the passenger, the ship's company were almost comparable to the famous gathering in the Arkansas tavern, and to them also there came a time when the suggestion was pertinent that they "all tell their real names." In later days there were even allusions to the fact that the passenger had three names, but these did not continue when it appeared that Mr. Bram had four. The passenger suffered under still graver inconveniences than that; his home was in America's most superior suburban town, and he had studied at a University which used to be regarded with suspicion in centers of perfect democracy. Beliefs have changed a little in thirty years; the public career of Harvard's most distinguished graduate of recent times, and the frequent success of her football elevens against those from cities where liberty, equality and fraternity were supposed to be rampant, have weakened the ancient myths. But not so long ago, even in a Massachusetts court or political meeting, any reference to Harvard was necessarily made in a tone of corroding sarcasm.

The *Fuller's* cargo of lumber included a deck-load, which is indicated on the plan. The deck-load, and the tops of the forward and after-houses made a new deck,

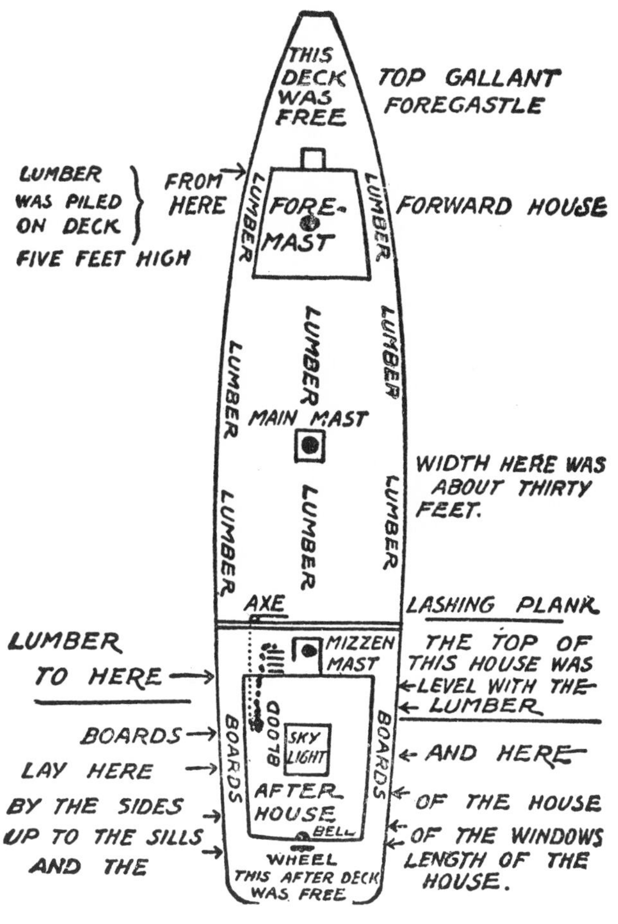


From "The Green Bag"

Deck of the *Fuller*

except in the bow and stern. She was towed down to Nantasket Roads on July 3, and was fog-bound there for five days. It must have been a tedious delay. The Captain returned to Boston, by the Hull steamer, for part of one day. The passenger was visited by his mother and sister. All the country were talking about silver and gold; New England's candidate for the Presidential nomination, Thomas B. Reed, had been defeated in the Republican convention, and Governor McKinley of Ohio was the nominee. Mr. Bryan's ill phrase had just been uttered, and was about to win him the leadership of his party for the first time. There was a Yale crew racing at Henley. And—some have thought this fact had a bearing upon the fortunes of the *Herbert Fuller*—the Cuban insurrection was going strong. The ship finally sailed on July 8.

The story of the next six days must be found in the evidence of eight or nine men of different degrees of intelligence, opportunities for observation, and interest in the outcome. Two juries, after long trials and long deliberations, did arrive at the same decision as to the main event, and while their verdicts probably gave less dissatisfaction than the verdict in the Borden trial, there are, as in that case, doubtful points, probably never to be explained. If the case for the Government was a strong one, and if it is impressive that it was twice sustained, it is also true that a powerful attack was made upon it, and that the length of time taken to arrive at an agreement, and the peculiar nature of the final verdict, indicate that there was hesitation, if not doubt,—a feeling which, in the minds of a few of those who remember the trial, has lingered until now. The reader of the narrative may be able to form an opinion whether there are any reasons for believing that a mistake was made, and made twice. The story as it appears in the testimony of the Government's witnesses, may be given first. The points which were contradicted by the accused man will be indicated later. As with the Borden murders, the limits of time and space closed in upon the commission of the crime; the murderer took long chances of being surprised at his work.

It was recorded, by most of the ship's company, that nothing especially unusual or disturbing happened on the *Herbert Fuller* for nearly a week. The captain and his wife, the two mates and the passenger had their meals together in the cabin, served by the steward. Mr. Monks borrowed Clark Russell's "A Voyage to the Cape" from the captain, read it, and discussed it with him. He lent him in return a new book of the year, Richard Harding Davis's "Three Gringoes in Venezuela and Central America." He was incautious enough to mention some of his yachting experiences to Mr. Bram, and wished he hadn't. That deep-sea mariner promptly made him aware of the ancient truth that the sailor looks upon the holiday yachtsman as if the latter belonged to the lesser and more detestable forms of parasitic life.

Spirituous and intoxicating drink play some part in the adventure; let us discuss what is known upon the subject. The second mate, it was reported by the steward, was drunk, on the ship, before sailing. He was never observed in that condition again, and aside from one other incident nothing else appears in this connection. Captain Nash was not a teetotaller, he was seen, at least once, "taking a drink," but it seems, literally, to have been one drink, and to have had no significance. The passenger brought on board two bottles of spirits, and sixty bottles of beer; apparently only a little of this had been consumed when the voyage ended.

The first mate, Mr. Bram, brought a two-gallon jug of whiskey, which, he said, was to be a present to a friend in Buenos Aires. But, if the *Fuller* had ever reached that port, the friend would have been disappointed, for by a distressing accident the jug was upset on deck before sailing, and all but two quarts were lost. This, said the mate, who was the sole witness to the catastrophe, accounted for the fact that when the steward, at a later period, emptied the jug, he found only about a pint of the whiskey. Mr. Bram's description of his own customs was simple: he never drank in the day time, but he took something when he turned in, or between watches at night. He seems to have told the passenger that the Captain did not care to have whiskey brought on board by any of his men, and on one occasion the young student gave both the mates a nip from his own meagre supply. The chief mate's hour for drinking was midnight, when John Jasper used to invoke the juice of the poppy, and when a damp chill settles upon the soul of him who works in the dark hours. Neither iced-water nor grape-juice make a cheering substitute for alcohol at that time.

Unless the crew of the barkentine engaged in a wicked conspiracy, there was one exception to the amiable conduct of those on board during the first days. This was the first mate, Mr. Bram. What he said and did might not have been remembered, had nothing else happened, but it is worth consideration. The seaman, Wassen, said that he heard loud, high words between the mates. Perdock heard them talking "loud" together; they were in the carpenter's shop at the time. He did not understand enough English to make out what they said. Slice was in the rigging, and observed that Bram and Blomberg were having a dispute. He could not hear their words. When, on the witness stand, he described this incident, it was inquired of him by the Court: "Dispute between whom?" And Slice, innocently adopting an ancient gag of the variety stage, replied: "Between the fore and main masts, sir!" And Mr. Justice Colt explained to this unconscious German comedian the difference between "who" and "what."

During the second day at sea, Loheac heard "high words" between the mates, and on the Saturday following heard the second mate say to Mr. Bram: "I wish you would let me go about my work." Later, Blomberg told Bram that he had been on a big ship, with twenty-four men in the crew. Bram's reply was that he didn't want to hear where the second mate had been, nor what he had done. Anderson heard the dispute in the carpenter's shop, and heard Blomberg say to Bram: "Don't try to run me; I know my business, and you mind your own business." Mere bickering, it is quite possible, and not of the greatest significance.

One man of the ship's company was conspicuous for his intelligence and resolution: the young mulatto steward, Spencer. Men talked to him, and, in some degree, confided in him. As he put it, he heard the mates "having a growl once or twice." But he heard more than that; he heard Bram say to the second mate: "That damn sarcastic talk of yours is the only thing I will kill a man for." The second mate made some inaudible reply, and Bram put him off with: "Don't you get excited. Don't you get excited." Bram, so said Spencer, talked to him about Captain and Mrs. Nash in a manner which was disrespectful at the least, and may have been something worse: an attempt to sound out the steward, and see how far he could be relied upon to join a mutinous outbreak against his employer. In the cabin, one day, Mrs. Nash asked the passenger what courses he had taken in college. The first mate came on deck afterwards, and asked the steward: "Did you hear what she asked him?" The steward assented, and Bram went on: "Any fool could ask that question . . . She is only putting on. She is nothing but a factory girl." The mate uttered more than one complaint to the steward (as well as to the passenger) that the captain was "mean,"—that is, too sparing with his money. Finally he said, as he was quoted by Spencer: "Here is a man that has got a good vessel, but don't take any care of her. He isn't deserving of her. Some other sport will dash his money up against the wall"—and the steward said, in interpretation of this phrase, "he didn't explain it that way, but he explained it vulgar." And the conclusion of the talk, as Spencer reported it, was the remark by Bram: "Captain Nash might die, and Mrs. Nash might get married to a young man, and that is just the way his money will go."

Was this the speech of a man whose mind was already

busy with wicked plots, or was it merely the loose-mouthed chatter of one who lived among rough men, and translated his black thoughts into nothing more harmful than windy conversation with a sea-cook? In lonely places, on ships and in camps, when time passes slowly, much empty talk has always been uttered; idle bluster about what might be done to rob this man of his money, or that one of his woman. Many dreadful threats have burst upon the air, like bubbles filled with gas,—representing the desire of feeble men to look like demons to their comrades. One great example in literature is that amazing scene among the raftsmen, in "Life on the Mississippi," as overheard by young Mr. Finn.

"But he didn't explain it that way," said the steward, "he explained it vulgar." This is typical of the fastidiousness of a ship's crew in which one member, Charley Brown, said that he could not sleep in the forecastle, but came up on deck, because of the "insects." The amusing delicacy of such men is one of the greatest surprises which one encounters in reading actual reports of their talk, and sometimes in listening to it. Gone are those purple patches of profanity which have given an awful and vicarious joy to refined readers looking for realism; those floods of Rabelaisian speech are nearly dried up. Of course, Charley Brown may have been less mincing when he talked with his ship-mates about those "insects." But I am quite ready to believe that he was not. Crude and unrefined speech, the bellowing oaths of the pirate, soldier and sailor, naughty language of all kinds, are becoming almost the exclusive possession of literary men,—and women. I do not see how the traditionally sulphurous diction of mule-drivers, stokers, cowboys and other romantic figures can be saved for their successors, unless they are all made to study the novels and see the plays of the realistic authors. For there alone, in the works of those who know the facts of life, and present them fearlessly, can these untutored folk learn how they ought to talk.

On Monday, July 13, the ship was about seven hundred and fifty miles from Boston, in 36° 07′ north latitude, and 53° 25′ west longitude. They were getting well out toward the middle of the Atlantic, in that part which lies between the northeastern coast of the United States and the shores of Portugal. The Gulf Stream was near, and the air warm. The wind was moderate and the sea smooth,—according to sailors' use of that term. Supper was served to those in the cabin at about half-past five, and after supper most of them came on deck. The Captain and his wife were walking arm in arm on the starboard side of the after house; the passenger was sitting amidships. The steward, who was also on deck, observed that the first mate approached the Captain and spoke to him. The conversation was not overheard, but at its end the mate said to the steward, or in his hearing: "That ain't natural,"—an unexplained remark, which was accompanied by an angry look toward the Captain. About an hour later the steward carried some food below for the officers' late supper, and helped Mrs. Nash regulate a lamp which hung over the table in the cabin. From eight until twelve o'clock was the starboard watch, —the deck in charge of the second mate, Slice at the wheel for the first two hours, until relieved by Wassen;

the other two men forward, on lookout. At midnight, eight bells, would come the port watch, when Mr. Bram would take charge, Charley Brown come to the wheel, and Loheac and Perdock come up from below and go on lookout forward. Charley Brown's trick at the wheel was from twelve to two, when he would be relieved by Loheac from two to four. The wind had sprung up; there was a fresh breeze on the starboard quarter. Nearly all sails were set, and the *Fuller* was sailing six or seven knots. She was considered to be making eight, because of the current. At nine o'clock there was a slight rain-squall, enough to bring the Captain on deck, to speak for a moment to the second mate. After this, Captain Nash went below, put out the light in the chart room, and lay down on his cot. The only light in his room was that which shone through from the partly-turned down lamp over the cabin table. Yet Henry Slice, who was at the wheel, said that looking through the small cabin window he saw the Captain lie down, and afterwards could see his legs up as far as the knees, as he lay there. That window will be discussed later; perhaps nothing on any ship was ever so measured, inspected, re-inspected and gazed through, as this 11 by 16 inch aperture in the after house of the *Herbert Fuller*. It appears near the wheel in the picture of the ship, and its position is also marked on the plan of the cabin.

The passenger went to bed a little after eight o'clock. To prevent a rattling, when the ship rolled, Mr. Monks locked the door of his room,—and as a result, he is alive today. The mates were on deck when he turned in, and the Captain was reading in the chart-room. At some time

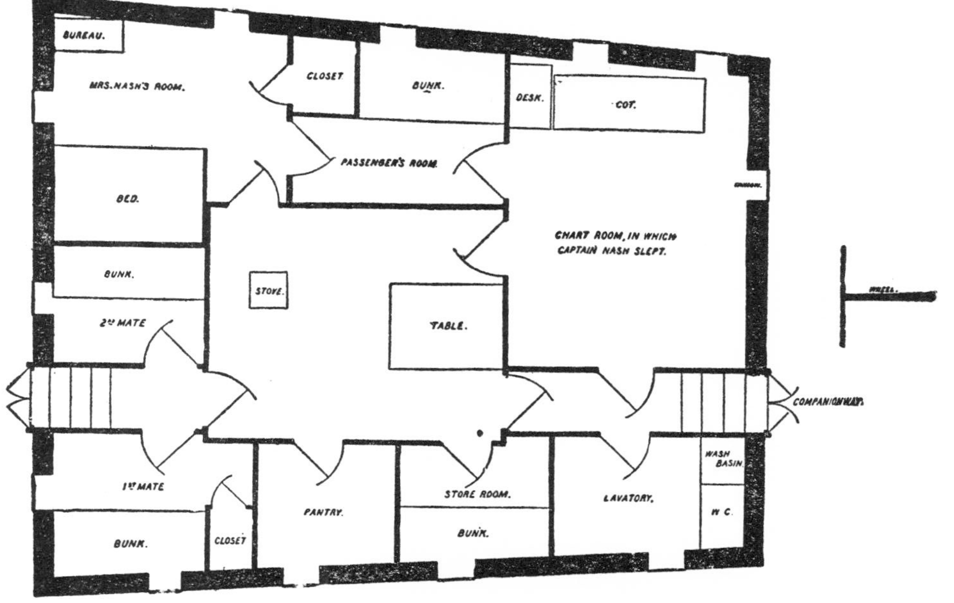


Plan of Cabin of the *Herbert Fuller*

in the night, he could not have told when, Mr. Monks was awakened by a scream,—the scream of a woman. Not wholly aroused at first, not wholly awake, and not sure, perhaps, what he had heard amid the creaks and groans of a ship at sea, he was sufficiently startled to listen, and presently he heard another sound, a "gurgling noise," coming from the chart-room. It was strange enough and alarming enough to awaken him completely; he twice called the Captain by name, but got no answer. He sat up, reached to a drawer underneath the bunk, and took from it a box of cartridges. He opened the box and loaded his revolver which had been kept under the pillow. Putting on a pair of slippers, he unlocked his door, and stepped into the chart-room. It was still dimly lighted from the lamp in the forward cabin. The Captain's cot was tipped over on one side, and the Captain himself lay on the floor, his breath rattling in his throat. The passenger called him by name again, but there was no reply. He put his hand on his shoulder, and found it wet with sweat. He went to call Mrs. Nash to the aid of her husband; her door leading from the forward cabin was open, but she could not be seen. On her bunk were what appeared to be splashes of blood, and, as the passenger said: "I suddenly realized that the scream I heard meant something."

He was alone in the dimly lighted cabin of a ship in mid-ocean; it was two o'clock in the morning, when courage is notoriously at a low ebb. All those about him had been strangers until a few days before. Some one had treacherously attacked the master of the vessel, who lay dying within a few feet. The Captain's wife, apparently, had been included in the attack. The passenger became aware that the cabin might be a most undesirable place in which to remain, and he resolved to get on deck. He started toward the stern, to go out by the after companionway, but thought that somebody might be standing on top of the companionway to strike at him as he came out. He turned and went to the forward companionway, looked up, and saw Bram, the chief mate, walking the deck between the main and mizzenmast.

He pointed his revolver toward him and called: "Mr. Bram!" The mate picked up a plank and threw it at him, but the plank fell across the hatchway and did not come inside. The passenger's statement as to this action with the plank was given explicitly at both trials, and also in a document signed at Halifax. In a paper signed on board ship the next morning, the phrase is merely "he picked up a board to throw at me," but the reason for this apparent discrepancy will be clear, I think, when the circumstances of the signing of this paper are explained. In Mr. Grinnell's account [1] of the first trial, it is said that "The mate took up the board and held it before him." Perhaps the best comment upon the incident was made by the United States Attorney at the first trial, and it was that the action of throwing the plank is no certain indication of what was in Bram's mind at the time. It is conceivable that a perfectly innocent man, seeing the passenger appear with an aimed revolver, would have done the same thing.

[1] See Appendix.

"Come below," called the passenger, "the Captain has been murdered. Come below, for God's sake!"

The mate answered: "No, no, no!" to which the passenger told him to come below and see for himself. Both together entered the cabin, and the mate, at the passenger's suggestion, went into his room and got a revolver. Then the passenger, going to his own room, changed his pyjamas for duck trousers and a flannel shirt. The mate waited outside Mr. Monks's room, and once started to go away, but was called back by the other. Captain Nash must have been unconscious, and was dying; the gurgling sound still came from his throat. Apparently neither of the living men knew what might be hidden in the shadows of the cabin; the passenger had not wholly recovered from his sudden awakening, and the horror of his two discoveries. If Bram, upon whom now devolved the command of the ship, was curious to learn what had happened, or desirous to help his dying Captain, he did nothing to show it. He did not, at this time, go near Captain Nash.

The two men returned to the deck, and sat down by the rail. Mr. Monks inquired for the second mate, arose, and said he was going to awaken him. The first mate said: "There is a mutiny. The second mate is forward with the crew." The passenger sat down again, and asked what o'clock it was. Bram replied that he did not know, and added a strange remark: that someone had set back the cabin clock. Then the mate began to cry, put his arms around the passenger's knees, and begged for protection. He had been hard on the crew, he said, and they would rush aft to kill him. The passenger promised to do what he could. The mate continued to talk; he felt sick, he explained, and he attributed this to a drink given him at twelve o'clock by the second mate, who said that he had procured the drink from Mr. Monks. The drink was in a tin cup, which had been thrown overboard by Blomberg. Bram said that he thought there had been some drug in the whiskey. Then he vomited upon the deck.[2]

The passenger suggested that Bram had better get up and walk about, so both rose and walked for five minutes. The mate staggered; the drink must have been a powerful one. Mr. Monks offered to go and wake the steward, but the mate objected. "If you do," said he, "somebody may rush at us around the forecastle house." Both sat down again; Bram faced aft, and the passenger forward. The mate covered the man at the wheel with his revolver, and the passenger kept his revolver pointing forward. He seems, at this time, to have accepted the story of the mutiny, although he informed Bram that he had not on this night or day given the second mate any drink. In this position, the two men waited the coming of daybreak.

Charley Brown had been relieved at the wheel by Loheac at some time around two o'clock, and before the passenger came on deck. It was the French sailor, therefore, who was steering the vessel, when there was enough daylight for anyone to be recognized. Before this, Mr. Monks had been unable to see anybody distinctly, although he made out the dim form of one of the lookouts.

[2] Readers of *The Wrecker*, Chapter XXIV, will be reminded of Captain Wicks's action.

When it was nearly day, the two went forward, rapped on the galley door, and wakened the steward. Spencer opened the door, clad only in a pair of trousers. He made a salute with his hand as a morning greeting; he was unprepared for the astonishing news.

"The Captain has been murdered," began the passenger.

This was a bit too much for the easy-going, but experienced steward.

"Oh, I guess not," he answered nonchalantly.

"Well, you can go and look for yourself," returned the passenger.

The three now started aft again, when Bram asked the steward if he had a revolver. Spencer replied: "No."

"Well, here," said the first mate, "you take this one," and put the weapon into the steward's hand. Spencer remarked that he was going to try it. He walked to the rail, and fired the revolver over the side. Bram jumped at the explosion, and it was afterwards discovered that all the remaining cartridges were nicked, as if they had been tried before.

Spencer looked through the skylight, and saw Captain Nash lying on the floor. Then he went around to the forward companionway, and descended to the cabin. He looked at the Captain's body for a moment. Then he saw the second mate's door was open, looked in, and found the officer lying in his bunk, with his feet crossed. His head was cut open, he was covered with blood, and one of his fingers was cut off. The steward ran on deck crying:

"The second mate has bled to death! Jesus Christ! What does this mean?"

The passenger turned to Bram.

"I thought you said the second mate was forward."

"Well," replied Bram, "he was forward."

They went to the man at the wheel, Loheac, covered him with their revolvers, and asked if he had heard or seen anything unusual in the night. He promptly said "No!" as might have been expected. Their next intention was to call the crew from below, but when they reached the main rigging on the starboard side, and stopped for a moment to consult, Bram suddenly pointed across the ship, and said:

"There is an axe. There is the axe that did it!"

The passenger and the steward looked in the direction indicated, but could see nothing. The mate's sight was better than theirs. They crossed the deck and found, half concealed under a lashing plank which bound the deck-load, a new axe, with blood on the head and handle. The steward picked it up, remarking:

"This is the axe that done it, this is the axe that killed the captain."

Bram took it from him, and borrowed his remark, saying again and again:

"This is the axe that done it!"

He wept and grinned hysterically over the axe, repeating the phrase more than once, and finally asked:

"Shall I throw it overboard?"

He had once given the passenger some good counsel; it now happened that the passenger unwittingly gave him some bad advice. Mr. Monks said:

"Yes; for fear the crew may use it against us."

The steward said "No," but it was too late. With another hysterical cry, the mate threw it into the ocean.

"You shouldn't have done that," Spencer told him,—and these were wise words.

The mate meditated, and the result was a suggestion.

"But we don't find no axe," said he.

The steward again was prompt and scornful.

"What do you take me for,—a God damn fool? Don't you know a man has seen you with the axe?"

He referred to the helmsman. But a definite suspicion had been formed in the mind of both passenger and steward. An unpleasant but significant incident took place while the three men were on deck together. Bram was clutching the steward, uttering dry sobs, and saying: "You will look out for me, take care of me, steward." He also repeated to the steward the story of the drugged whiskey. Spencer looked at the vomited matter on the deck, and said that he should collect some of it in a bottle and take it ashore for analysis. The mate then managed to slide into it in such a manner as to wipe it up,—and thereby, apparently, destroy another bit of evidence.

It must be remembered, in reading this, that the description of events is that given by Bram's shipmates, who afterwards became the Government witnesses against him. Their stories corroborate one another, although they differ in minor details, and sometimes vary as to the order in which incidents occurred,—naturally enough. So that the reader may consider the case, as the juries considered it, Bram's own account will be given later, and it may be seen how far he denied, explained, or gave a different interpretation to their testimony. With what has already been related, and with what is to come, must be remembered the plight in which these men found themselves at daybreak on July 14. A sudden attack—diabolically brutal and apparently senseless —had resulted in the death, while they slept, of three unoffending persons. It could not have come from outside: the murderer was still there, on board the ship, and when all had been assembled, they were talking with him, associating with him. He was going about with them, pretending to help discover the truth, and hiding his guilt, or his homicidal mania, which might break out at any moment. Each may well have suspected all the others. It is not a cause for wonder if many things which were said and done represented nobody's sincere convictions, but mere temporizing policy, the result of their situation.

The story of the *Herbert Fuller* has often been compared with the plots of some of Clark Russell's novels. A frequent situation in these novels is the truce after a mutiny, or other outbreak. Sometimes it is between the mutinous crew and the only officer left alive who can navigate the ship; in other stories it is between the under officers or the crew, and the captain, who is either insane or otherwise dangerous. But the underlying motive is the necessity for a navigator. For the safety of all, the skipper must have freedom of action to bring the ship into sight of port.

Precisely what had happened in the cabin of the *Fuller* between one and two o'clock on that morning will never be told. The blood-stained axe which had been found on deck and thrown overboard was a new one with a short handle. It had hung in the store-room opening from the cabin, and while its existence was known to all in the cabin, it is unlikely that any of the others on board had seen it. It is impossible to do more than guess what purpose moved him who had gone softly into the store-room and taken the axe from its place on the wall. The Captain and the second mate were both large men, and must have been heavy sleepers. It would have been the murderer's care to slaughter them first. Probably they had no conscious moment between sleep and death; no cry was heard from either. The murderer may then have tried the passenger's door; and found it locked. He then went to Mrs. Nash's room, and it is the attack on this poor woman which affects one's imagination most horribly. She lived to be conscious of her deadly peril, to scream, to try to rise in her bed, and pitifully to attempt to shield herself from the blows, as her gashed and wounded arms and hands made clear. As she had time to realize, this was not an imaginary terror of the night, one of the hideous visions which now and again bring unlucky mortals from sleep to waking, with a dread so real that men, in their waking hours, and in actual danger, have sometimes stayed motionless, thinking that they were merely in the grip of a nightmare. She screamed once, and half-awakened the passenger. Had he been wholly roused, he might have rushed out, met the murderer leaving Mrs. Nash's room, and have been killed himself, at that instant.

The murderer, gorged with blood, like the frightful

creature in the story of "Dracula," rushed on deck, and tried to conceal the weapon. For what purpose? Did he keep it for still more murderous work, or for his own defence? Were all these the unreasoning actions of a maniac, as it was afterwards contended, or the execution of a deliberate plot, formed in cool sobriety, but carried out under the impulsion of alcohol? If the latter, why was the plot, whatever it was, suddenly abandoned? Did the murderer over-rate his own courage,—plunge his hands deep in blood, and then draw back, terrified and hysterical, and from the most dangerous being on the ship, become the most abject? Was the inability to kill the passenger the beginning of the failure of the scheme, or was it that the butchery, in which he embarked, proved more than his physical strength could bear?

After Loheac had been confronted and questioned, the three men went forward and called the rest of the crew on deck. They were asked when they had last seen the second mate, and were informed of the murders. As they stood in a circle, the first mate began again to whimper. He said that both he and the Captain were Freemasons, and he made a touching reference to his "poor, old mother." The passenger slapped him on the shoulder and told him to brace up. Then the crew, except for the man at the wheel, went down into the cabin. They looked at the gashed body of the second mate for a moment; the passenger turned and went on deck, thinking that he had had enough. They entered the room of Mrs. Nash, and found her lying on the bed. The bones of the skull were broken in front and back, her jaws were smashed, and her hands and arms badly wounded. She was in her nightgown, which was pushed up to her knees. Charley Brown tried to cover the body more completely, and pulled the garment down. Then this terrified and puzzled group of sailors looked at the body of their Captain as he lay in the chart-room. There were seven or eight wounds in his head; the brain had been penetrated twice. Mr. Bram was again affected to sorrow, if not to tears, and said: "Look at the Captain,—I'd die for him." The offer had come somewhat too late.

They all returned to the deck, and the first mate began to make suggestions and tentative offers, rather than to issue commands.

"You will stand by me, boys, won't you?" he asked. He suggested shaking hands, and some of them shook hands with him. But his first plan was not received with favor.

"Well, now," said he, "we will take those bodies out of there and throw them overboard, and wash up the blood in the cabin."

But Slice, the dogged German, who appears to have had a good bit of sense, did not agree.

"We doesn't throw the bodies overboard, we must take them in as evidence; and we doesn't clean the cabin out either, we must leave it just as it is."

And all hands agreed. Slice made the further suggestion that they lash the jolly-boat amidships, put the bodies in it, and cover the boat with tarred canvas.

"We can take the bodies home as evidence and save them for the family at the same time."

Anderson saw Bram "praying to God, and putting his hands up above his head, and saying that the Captain was a Freemason and he was a Freemason." Slice said that Bram acted "excited" and "looked flushed in the face,"—but so, possibly, did all. No complete report of all that was said has ever been made; nobody knows what was surmised and suspected. Some little attempt was made at cheer and human companionship; a box of the passenger's cigars was brought on deck and passed around.

"We all here is one," genially suggested Mr. Bram.

His conduct seems to have resembled that of many "peace-loving" folk, who think that both evil and danger may be overcome by the simple process of ignoring them. He advanced a theory that the two dead men had killed Mrs. Nash and each other in a fight which had concerned her, and he added:

"We must not blame the living for the dead, the dead can't speak for themselves."

As Mr. Grinnell wrote, Bram spoke and acted "as if it were not an uncommon thing anywhere to have three murders before breakfast on a week day." To shake hands all round and forget the past seems to have been the philosophy of this blithe optimist. It should not be sneered at by any of the good and learned folk who, when the world was drenched in blood, advocated the same easy method of cleaning up. Throw the dead overboard, blame everything upon them, and go forward light-heartedly into the future. Take heed for the innocent and defenceless who again may suffer, if you leave the beast of prey at large? By no means. And those who utter the antiquated word "justice," or those who believe in taking measures for further protection against violent men or violent nations, can easily be rebuked by gently cautioning them not to indulge in "hatreds."

The curious but convenient notion that the dead alone were guilty, was advanced in different forms and for various reasons. It may be well to anticipate a little, and give it in its most engaging version, as it was related on the witness-stand by that peculiar seaman, Charley Brown. He said that he overheard a conversation, that morning, between Mr. Bram and Mr. Monks. One of them—he did not remember which one—advanced a theory as to the murders, which he undertook to reconstruct from the depths of his strange memory. He then repeated it in his defective English and this was it:

"The second officer, Mr. Blamberg, intend to go in and insult Mrs. Nash, and Captain Nash come out to see him. Captain Nash take the axe to kill his wife, and then he intend to kill the second mate, and the second mate having been a stronger man than Captain Nash, the second mate have overpowered Captain Nash and kill him, and after that the second mate had struck himself with the axe and walked out on the deck load and put that axe, and walked from there back to his bed, and lied down and died."

After this it is not surprising to read in the stenographic report of the trial the comment:

"(Laughter)"

"The Crier: Order!"

Before the bodies were brought on deck, the passenger found, or was shown spots of blood coming up the forward companionway, and leading across the top of the after house (which was painted white) to a place where.

instead of drops was a broad stain of blood, as if the axe had lain there. Other, smaller drops led forward to the lashing plank, where the axe had been found.

Charley Brown went into the second mate's cabin and brought out the officer's sewing bag which was stained with the owner's blood. Some of the blood got on Brown's clothes,—a fact to which he called the attention of his ship-mates. The bodies of the two men were brought on deck, by a number of the crew, and sewed up in sheets and towels by Brown. The passenger took the wheel while the men were engaged in this work. Mrs. Nash's body was sewed into the bed-clothes in her room, so that the dead woman should not be exposed to the sight of the whole crew. The three bodies were placed in the boat, and before the canvas cover was fastened over it the passenger said that he thought it would be proper to read the burial service. This made an instant appeal to the emotions of Mr. Bram, who expressed a wish to have music at the ceremony. He suggested that they bring up the organ from the cabin. But the passenger, with that dislike for demonstrations of this kind, which we are often told is one of the grave defects in the New Englander's character, said: "No, that is foolishness." One of the sailors then took the wheel, the rest of the crew gathered around the boat, with their hats in their hands, while the passenger read, from the Book of Common Prayer, the Order at the Burial of the Dead at Sea. I have read many stories about the ocean, but I do not recall any scene like that.

Afterwards they adventured upon more perilous ground; they embarked upon literary composition. Mr.

Bram suggested that they draw up an account of the crime, and asked the passenger to do it. Mr. Monks wrote the following bothersome document:

Tuesday, July 14, 1896.

Monday night everything on board of the barkentine *Herbert Fuller* was perfectly quite and peaceful. The crew had no fault to find with anything on board. The second mate had the watch from 8 until 12. I went to bed about 8 o'clock. The steward says the captain had been drinking, but I did not notice it. I am naturally a very heavy sleeper, so the murders which were committed might have happened before I woke up.

My first recollections are these: I heard a scream, followed by a gurlling noise, as if someone was choking. I reached down and got a box of shells, took my revolver and filled the pistol, which I kept under my pillow, as fast as possible. Then I called, "Captain Nash." As I got no answer I unlocked my cabin door and stepped out into the after cabin.

The captain slepted on a cot placed against the starboard wall. The captain was lying on the floor with the couch tipped upon end. I went up to him and shook him. I found he was covered with blood. I ran into Mrs. Nash's room to call her.

I could see that sheets of her bunk were covered with blood. I then ran forward to the forward companion way and looked on the deck. I saw the mate, Mr. Bram, on deck. I called to him and held my revolver pointed toward him.

When he saw me, he picked up a board to throw at me, but I called out: "It's me—Mr. Monks; come below for God's sake."

He came below, and we took the lantern in the foreward cabin and went into the after cabin. I slipped on a pair of trousers and a shirt; he grabbed his revolver, and we ran on deck. We did not know who were our friends or foes. We crouched down on the deck to windard just abreast of the mizzenmast.

Mr. Bram covered the man at the wheel, and I kept my revolver pointed forwards. It was very dark. In this way we sat waiting for daylight. We then—

(Then written above a line across the page is: "We found a bloody axe on the deck which we threw overboard, as we feared the crew would use it against us." And then the sentence goes on from the first page.)

We then went forward and banged on the galley door for the steward, J. Spencer. He came on deck, and we told him what had happened. He went aft and went into the cabin, while Bram and myself kept on deck with our revolvers.

He came running out of the cabin in a few minutes and said the (something scratched out) second mate, Mr. Blum, was lying dead in his birth. We then went aft in a body and questioned the man at the wheel. He said he didn't know anything had happened, and had heard no unusual noises.

We then went forward and woke up the crew.

They all appeared greatly astonished and all protested they knew nothing.

We all then went aft in a body and went into the cabin. The second mate was lying dead in his bunk. Mrs. Nash was lying in her bunk with her clothes pulled up. Captain Nash was lying on the floor dead. We went on deck and at once decided to steer for French Cayane, that being the nearest port.

My theory of the tragedy is this:—

The second mate, Mr. Blum, had been drinking, and went below and tried to rape Mrs. Nash. Captain Nash woke up and went and got an ax (the one we threw overboard) and attempted to kill Blum and his wife. Blum must off gotten the axe and hit the captain and then staggered on deck and then back to his bunk.

Lester Hawthorne Monks.

The second mate offered Mr. Bram a drink at about 12 o'clock. This whiskey made Mr. Bram very sick while on deck with me, and he acted as if he had been drugged.

Lester Hawthorne Monks.
Thomas H. Bram, Mate.
Jonathan Spencer.
Charles Brown.
Frank Loheac.
Falke Wassin.

On the back:

"Henry J. Slice, Oscar Andersson, Hendrik Perdok."

This paper survived to plague everybody connected with it. The author of it had to undergo much heckling in court as to why he spelled as he did. He admitted that he was not a good speller, and suggested that the attorney who questioned him might have been a little inaccurate if he had been on the *Fuller* that morning. This, the cross-examiner readily admitted, but still persisted in his questioning, with the object, evidently, of showing that Mr. Monks was nervous and excited. Whether this was to impeach his reliability as a witness, or to raise the suspicion that the passenger might have imagined the murders, is not perfectly clear. And no one in court pointed out that spelling, like a gift for mathematics, is no great accomplishment in itself, and while a student from a scientific school was not correct in spelling, neither was Robert Louis Stevenson at the height of his literary career.

More serious than the matter of spelling, however, was the question why some of these men signed a document which they knew or suspected must be absurd. The reason was that they were all dissembling; playing for time; wondering about the truth, but trying to avoid letting anybody know that he was suspected. Three of them, including the passenger and the steward, had very definite suspicions indeed. The steward said that he declared, at the time the paper was brought to him:

"That ain't so; them people didn't kill themselves; nothing of the kind."

Pressed as to why he signed, he continued:

"I signed it because I didn't want them to know that I knew as much as I did; didn't want to be too smart;

signed it more for peace than anything else. I didn't want them to think that I doubted what they said."

He also admitted that he felt that he might be the next one to be attacked by the murderer; doubtless everybody on board believed that all were in danger. Nobody took much sleep at night; the passenger and the steward thought that for six days and nights they had altogether only about six hours' sleep each.

The voyage to Rosario was abandoned, and it was agreed that they must make the nearest port. Mr. Bram said that this was Cayenne in French Guiana, and the course was altered for that place. It was pointed out, however, that this was 1500 miles distant. Bermuda was considered, as only about 400 miles away. But the wind was dead ahead, and the final decision was for Halifax, or St. John, for which they had a favoring wind. A course was then taken for Halifax. It has been said, in favor of the first mate, now the commanding officer, that he was the only navigator on board, and that he could have taken the ship anywhere he pleased. But he did not assume any decided command; either he fell in promptly with the suggestions of others; or he showed but a feeble and fleeting opposition to the decisions of seamen, steward and passenger. The reasons for this furnish an entertaining problem in what our grandfathers called human nature, and what we, with an almost sickening iteration, term psychology.

Mr. Bram appointed Charley Brown and Frank Loheac as first and second mates respectively. Bram and Charley were now nominally, at least, first and second in command of the *Fuller*,—which, in view of their status when the ship arrived in port, was an ironic circumstance. Some time during the day Brown threw overboard a pair of overalls, stained with the blood and dirt accumulated during his work on the bodies. On that day also, according to Mr. Grinnell, the steward made the direct remark to the passenger: "The mate killed them people." This would hardly appear in testimony and I do not find it there. The handles were cut off the tools in the carpenter's shop, and the shop nailed up. The cabin was shut and locked. On Wednesday night the crew were made to sleep on deck, or on the after house. Late that afternoon the passenger had told Mr. Bram that one of the sailors had told Spencer and himself that Charley Brown had changed his clothes on the night of the murder. The three agreed that this was suspicious, and they decided to put Brown in irons next morning. Some of the sailors thought that Brown's conduct had strangely altered since the murders. He had become moody and reticent; he changed color when anybody looked at him. The crew were assembled, and searched for weapons by Spencer and Bram, as the Captain's revolver was missing. On Thursday, as Brown lay asleep on the forward house, Spencer, Monks, and Bram went forward, Spencer jumped on him and held him down, while Bram ran to the cabin and fetched a pair of irons. Charley was then manacled. He asked:

"What is this for?" but made no resistance. Asked why he had changed his clothes on Monday night, he said that it was because he was cold.

Mr. Bram, after first asking the passenger to do it, wrote this account of the event.

Wednesday, day of 15 July, 1896.

On this day, at 5.30 P.M., the steward of said H. Fuller came to me and told me that the sailors all came and made an open statement to him in reference to one of the sailors whose name is Charles Brown's conduct of guilt in regard to the murder which took place on board said vessil. I at once got each men's statement; then upon the strength of these statements we came to the conclusion to put him in irons at daybreak. At 7 p m all hands was musterd aft and thoroughly searcht. No other wepon was given them but their knives. Each man was then placed a certin distance apart from each other untop of the after house. Myself, the steward and passenger was stationed amidships well armed, and kept a good lookout untile daybreak. At 5 a m Charles Brown was mancled and put in irons. His actions all night was very suspicious and got himself all ready, as it were, to jump over the side, but he was well guarded by all hands on board. At 1.30 a. m. he made an effort rush for the forward part of the ship, but was instantly stop by the steward upon a pointed revolver towards him.

Thomas M. Bram, Mate,
Jonathan Spencer, Steward,
Lester Hawthorne Monks,
Frank Loheac,
Folke Wassene,
Oscar Andersson,
Henry Slice.

The word "effort" used in describing the "rush" which Brown had made forward, was in Bram's first version, written as "desprate." The change was made at the suggestion of the passenger, who declared that there was nothing desperate in Brown's action. The sailor's motive in trying to go forward had turned out to be quite innocent. The steward, when he fell upon him, cursed him for a robber and charged him with stealing the Captain's revolver. Brown mildly replied: "Oh, steward, you do wrong!" The revolver was afterwards found, where the Captain had left it.

Mr. Bram said to the passenger:

"Now that we have got the murderer, we will tear up the paper that you wrote."

But Mr. Monks replied:

"We don't know that we have got the murderer, and we won't tear it up. We will keep it."

The time passed in general wretchedness, fear and suspicion. The nights were cold for sleeping on deck, and getting colder as they sailed northward. The days, however, were hot, and by Saturday the smell of the bodies had become so unbearable that it was resolved to lower the boat, and tow it astern. This was accordingly done.

Bram talked to Wassen, and said:

"If we don't get Brown guilty we will get two years each."

On Saturday morning there fell a flat calm; they sighted land which they supposed to be Sable Island. They had seen one or two distant vessels, hull down, and beyond communication. Now they sighted a steamship; an English tramp. She came toward them, and the passenger proposed to signal her.

"What good will it do?" inquired Mr. Bram.

"Well," returned the other, "we can get a navigator on board."

"Don't you think I am good enough navigator?"

"No," was the answer.

"Well, if we signal her, it will take all the glory away from us."

Mr. Monks remarked that he did not care anything about glory: what he wished was to get ashore.

They brought up the fog-horn and sounded it. Mr. Bram was asked to look up the code signal for "Mutiny; want assistance." He took the signal book but made no progress in finding the signal, so the passenger looked it up, and the flags were hoisted. The steward climbed the mizzen rigging and waved a large sheet. The national ensign was run up, union down, in sign of distress. The steamer stopped her engines, and lay to for about half an hour, regarding them. Finally she started her engines and steamed away. Perhaps the multiplicity of signals made the Englishman suspect that all this was but an injudicious display of American humor. At sundown the *Fuller* caught a breeze, and during the night ran into fog.

Sunday noon Anderson came to the passenger with an amazing story. He and others had been talking with Charley Brown, who had been kept in a hole formed by the lumber around the mizzenmast. Brown said that on the night of the murders, while he was at the wheel, shortly before two o'clock, he had heard a noise in the chart-room. Looking through the window in the after house he had seen the mate, striking at someone who lay on the cot beneath. He could not see who was sleeping there, and had supposed that it was the passenger. A short time later he heard the shriek from Mrs. Nash's room. Then he saw Bram come up on deck again by the forward companionway. He thought that he was about to be attacked himself, and was in terror for his life. His fear had not wholly vanished during the hours and days that followed, and this accounted for his changed demeanor.

It will, of course, be remarked that this was told by a man who was himself under arrest for the crime. But, combined with the other highly suspicious circumstances, it carried conviction, and they resolved to put Bram in irons. As he sat on the after house, facing aft, the steward approached him from behind and seized him by the shoulders. Like Brown he made no resistance, but said:

"What is this for?"

"For killing the Captain," replied Spencer.

"I am innocent, steward," was the reply, and his face turned a deeper red.

The steward covered him with a revolver, when Bram said:

"Don't ill-treat a man; I am innocent."

He was ironed, and secured near the mainmast.

The fog cleared on Sunday afternoon, and that night they observed the flash of a light-house which indicated that they were off Beaver Island, about sixty miles above Halifax. By Monday noon the fog closed in again, and they found themselves in the midst of a fishing fleet.

They spoke a fisherman and got their course and the distance. The weather continued thick, and they had to stand out to sea again until daybreak on Tuesday, July 21. Then they sighted a pilot, who came aboard, heard their story, and took command. The voyage of the *Herbert Fuller* had ended. She entered the harbor of Halifax, towing a boat which carried the dead bodies of her Captain, her second officer, and the Captain's wife. Her present commander and first officer were in irons on deck under suspicion of murder. The rest of the crew were in fear and confusion, half dead from weariness and lack of sleep. And now they faced the endless questionings of police, port officers, the officials of the American consulate, and the newspaper reporters.

Some account of the voyage and the murders appeared next day on the front page of almost every newspaper in North America. The phrase, "murder on the high seas," caught everyone's fancy. The water-fronts buzzed with the sensational story. All who lived near the sea were especially interested, and launched upon discussions of the *Herbert Fuller*, upon talk about Captain Nash, about Bram, Brown, Monks and Spencer, talk which was to develop into a controversy, and to last for months and years. That happy summer I had nothing more serious to do than to sail about the mouth of one of the New England rivers in a little dory, and I can recall the eagerness with which all the men who lived on or near the water took up the discussion, and followed the news as it developed day by day, as the crew of the *Fuller* were brought back from Halifax to the port of her departure.

There was the delay, usual to American criminal law, before the case came to trial. One of the reasons why murder is not an extra-hazardous occupation in the United States, why there is such a disproportion between the number of homicides and the number of convictions, is that by the time the accused person is brought before a jury the horror felt at the crime has faded and disappeared. The prisoner has become the center of a pity often quite misplaced. It is then easy for newspapers which are edited for semi-intelligent persons with maudlin sympathies to represent the accused man or woman as the victim of persecution by the police, who, during the course of the trial, are aided by one or two remorseless attorneys for the Government. This condition of affairs was more noticeable in two other trials recorded in this book than in the Bram case, but it is rare, in any conspicuous murder trial, if the attorney for the people does not find himself assailed as a public enemy, merely because he is faithful to his trust.

The Grand Jury found an indictment against Mr. Bram, but not against Charley Brown. The latter then joined his ship-mates, who were being held as witnesses in the Charles Street Jail. The passenger and the steward, as responsible persons, were released, one on his personal recognizance and the other on bail. But the rest of the men of the *Herbert Fuller*, with the usual fate of the poor and friendless, had to stay in confinement, to test the truth of Dr. Johnson's observation about the superiority of life in jail to that on board ship. There is no doubt that they were safer and better paid than they would have been at sea.

The crimes had been committed in an American ship, on the high seas, and so the trial was not in a State court, but before the Circuit Court of the United States,—for the First Circuit, in Boston. The Justices were Circuit Judge Colt and District Judge Webb. The United States District Attorney, Sherman Hoar, Esq., and his assistants, John H. Casey, Esq., and Frederick P. Cabot, Esq., represented the Government, and the counsel who had been assigned to the defence, James E. Cotter, Esq. and Asa P. French, Esq. appeared for the prisoner.[3] The trial began on December 14, 1896, and was of extraordinary interest, for a number of reasons.

The jury saw the murderer, and heard him testify—whoever he was. Everybody left alive in the *Herbert Fuller* appeared in court and gave evidence. There was no question of some unknown outsider; no "wild-eyed man," nor stray tramp could be blamed for the crimes. The jury saw the whole ship's company, and could decide who was telling truth, and who was concealing guilt. There are no degrees of murder in a United States Court; the accused was either guilty of murder or he was not, and if the former, there was at the time of this first trial, no punishment except death by hanging. All the seamen except one, all persons who were forward on the ship between one and two o'clock on the morning of July 14, were soon excluded from suspicion. This left three men who were near the scene of the murders: the first mate, the passenger, and the man at the wheel. The passenger was soon excluded, after a few vague insinuations were made about him in cross-examination. The writer for-

[3] Henry S. Ormsby was later associated with the defence.

merly quoted, Mr. Grinnell, who was present at both trials, summed up on this point as follows:

"There was no evidence against Monks. It does not appear that anyone on board ever suspected him. Bram swore at the trial that he never had suspected Monks. The bearing of Monks at the trial was unexceptionable. He endured a torturing cross-examination in a manner which probably strengthened the jury's belief in his testimony."

The other notable points in the trial were the powerful attack made by the defence upon Charley Brown, directly charging him with guilt; the testimony of a detective from Halifax; the attempt of the prosecution to introduce evidence about a former voyage of Bram's; the testimony of the prisoner himself; and the evidence of expert witnesses upon a question of seamanship.

Nicholas Power, a detective officer from Halifax, testified, under objection by the defence, that he questioned Bram in his own office. Mr. Bram was then in custody. This conversation took place:

"Bram, we are trying to unravel this horrible mystery. Your position is rather an awkward one. I have had Brown in this office and he made a statement that he saw you do the murder."

Bram replied: "He could not have seen me; where was he?"

"He states he was at the wheel."

"Well, he could not see me from there."

"Now, look here, Bram, I am satisfied that you killed the Captain, from all I have heard from Mr. Brown. But some of us think that you could not have done all that crime alone. If you had an accomplice you should say so, and not have the blame of this horrible crime on your own shoulders."

The close of the talk was Bram's reply:

"Well, I think and many others on board of the ship think that Brown is the murderer, but I don't know anything about it."

The first two of Bram's answers contain something which looks perilously close to an admission, but it proved to be unfortunate for the Government that this witness was allowed to testify.

The prosecution made no direct charge of motive, and the apparent purposeless nature of three such murders has been a puzzle to some of those who have heard of the case. It was freely charged outside the court, and widely believed that Bram had long entertained piratical ambitions—was a sort of spiritual descendant of the old sea-robbers of his native isle, St. Kitts. The theory was that he intended to seize the ship and sell her,—perhaps to the Cuban insurgents. While the United States Attorney, Mr. Hoar, offered no direct evidence as to this design, he did endeavor to introduce a witness named Nicklas, from Baltimore, the first mate of the schooner *White Wings*, of which Bram had been second mate. Mr. Nicklas was to testify that on one voyage Bram had proposed to him that they kill the Captain, seize and sell the ship and cargo. Nicklas laughed at the suggestion. Bram thereupon had said:

"If you don't want to kill this particular Captain, let us go on board a Norwegian vessel where they have fewer men before the mast, where they don't talk our language, and where they are laden with coffee . . . We can give the crew knockout drops . . . and then kill the Captain, and the crew of the vessel will obey our orders."

Nicklas was still unbeguiled by this seductive plan. Bram told him, so he said, that he had twice engaged in certain acts of hocus-pocus, which did not include murder: once on the *Twilight*, of which he was Captain and part owner, when he collected the freight money and sank the vessel, explaining to the other owners that the money went down with the ship. The other concerned a cargo of cocoanuts which he carried into Belize in the schooner *China*. He pretended that the cargo had been ruined by water, when, as a matter of fact, he had disposed of it, uninjured, for a sum of money which he pocketed.

In the absence of the jury the prosecution argued for the admission of Nicklas' testimony, and cited numerous cases, including the celebrated Australian case of Makin. In this, the defendant also had an unfortunate habit or custom: that of living in houses where some evil-disposed person had buried babies in the back-yard. But, I believe, it is almost hopeless to attempt to introduce this kind of evidence in an American court, and in this case it was promptly excluded. (Similar testimony, admitted at the first Molineux trial, caused a reversal.) When his career on the *White Wings* was reached in the cross-examination of Bram, and Mr. Hoar asked why he had been discharged from that vessel, the defence promptly and properly objected. Again there was a recess, while counsel argued the point before the justices in the lobby. The Government produced a certificate from the American Vice-Consul at Rio, saying that Bram had been discharged at that port "on complaint of the Master, R. E. M. Davisson, that he had well founded suspicions of said Bram having intentions to steal the vessel." The date of this is significant: February 1, 1896, only a few months before the sailing of the *Fuller*, and the alleged plot to seize that ship. But the Court excluded all this testimony. It may be said that the defence had intimated that it would impeach the character of Nicklas, if he were allowed to give evidence. But it is not clear how the certificate of the Vice-Consul could be explained away.

Two of the most important witnesses for the Government were the passenger and the steward. The substance of this testimony has been given in the story of the voyage. It was only Charley Brown who claimed to have been a direct witness of one of the murders, and this fact he had not divulged until he was under arrest.

> "He was of short stature," writes Mr. Grinnell, "with fair hair and a great moustache, from behind which sounded a voice trained to do service in storms. A large, muscular neck held his head up straight and tossed it back now and then as he talked. His manner was that of a seafaring man who had ceased to expect luck, and was not enthusiastic in the hope of justice. There was no pretension to virtue above the habits of his class. He spoke freely of the time when in Rotterdam 'I lost my money and my girl.' He admitted that he

> lied in telling yarns. He seemed to be a man who could and would tell the truth in emergencies, and he gave the impression that he was telling it on the stand. It was an impressive moment in the court-room when he was asked whom he saw striking the captain, and he, looking straight at the prisoner, replied with a tone of solemn energy, 'Mate Bram.' "

Charley Brown testified that he came to the wheel, on that night, at eight bells, twelve o'clock. He saw Bram walking the deck forward of the after house. He would see him for a while, and then lose him from sight in the darkness. Finally, after Bram had disappeared for the third time, he heard a noise from the cabin. Looking through the window he saw the cot upset, and saw the lower half of a man's body lying on the floor. At the time he did not know it was the Captain. The mate, Bram, was standing over him, striking at him with some weapon of which he saw only the handle. Bram was easily recognizable; for one reason, because he wore a straw-hat with a hole cut in the crown which the witness had often seen before. After this Brown heard the shriek from Mrs. Nash's room, and then saw the mate return to the deck.

In cross-examination of Brown, the defence began to uncover an astonishing story; one which shook the case for the prosecution, and for a time, seriously threatened it. Brown, it appeared, about five years earlier, had landed from a ship in Antwerp after a long voyage from Tacoma. He had been paid off, at the end of the voyage, in sovereigns, fifty-five pounds in English gold. Planning to go to Copenhagen to see his family, he had taken a train for Rotterdam, but in the train began to "feel sick." He said he was "scared about everybody I see around me in the railroad" and thought they were going to do him some harm; to steal his money. He left the train at Rotterdam, and secured a room for the night. He was unable to sleep at first; then he lost consciousness and came to himself in a hospital. He had been out of his head, he was told, for fourteen days, and while in that condition, when somebody entered his room, he had fired a revolver, the shot going through the window. His money had disappeared. He admitted giving an embroidered version of this to some of his ship-mates in the *Fuller;* in that account he said he had *killed* a man in Rotterdam. He had also suggested to Loheac that by upsetting a barrel of kerosene which lay in the fore peak, and touching a match to it, the destruction of the *Fuller* might be accomplished.

The Rotterdam incident had not been unknown before, and it had been investigated. But on the day when Brown was testifying, the defence produced a document just received from the American Consul in Rotterdam. This enclosed a statement from the Commissioner of Police in that city giving a longer and more damaging account of Brown's adventure, than had been told in court up to that moment. The junior counsel for the defence, Mr. French, during a moment of great excitement in court, charged Brown with perjury, and asked for a postponement for further investigation, with an intent to bring certain witnesses from Holland. Brown was recalled to the stand, examined still further by the Government, and the story was elicited as it is given above. The defence urged that the document indicated that Charley had a mania of persecution, or of "pursuit," and was, in fact, a homicidal maniac, and alone of all on board the *Fuller* capable of committing the crimes. The Government answered that they proposed to corroborate Brown on every point except the assertion that he actually witnessed one of the murders. The Court denied the motion for postponement, and the trial proceeded.

It is, of course, a strong point for the defence when the accused person takes the witness stand in his own behalf. Bram testified and was cross-examined at great length. He told of his own career on other ships and in the Dennett restaurants. When he came to the crucial moment—two o'clock on the morning of July 14—he said that he heard a sound, and saw Brown at the mizzen peak jig. He walked aft, and Brown returned to the wheel. (He did not, apparently, question Brown as to why he had left the wheel.) Then he saw Brown putting on his slippers,—the inference being that Brown, for some reason, had been going about in his stocking feet. A few minutes later, looking down the forward companionway, he saw Mr. Monks with his revolver. He picked up the board as a shield; he did not throw it. They went into the cabin together; he heard the gurgling noise from the Captain, and imitated it for the benefit of the jury. He felt of the Captain's feet, to see if he were dead. He proposed going into Mrs. Nash's room, but the passenger discouraged the idea. He accounted for his nausea by the sight he had seen in the cabin. He said that the story of the fight between the Captain and the second mate about Mrs. Nash originated with the passenger. He claimed that the steward first saw the axe, and that the suggestion to throw it overboard came from the passenger and was joined in by the steward. He asked each man if he knew anything about the murder, and when all had denied it, he said:

"Well, if that is the case, I can't blame anybody for this occurrence. The people are dead and they cannot answer for themselves, and God only knows how it occurred."

As to his weeping, and use of strange expressions when the Captain's body was brought on deck, he admitted that he did weep. He said he gave the distress signal of a Mason, as he and the Captain both belonged to that fraternity, and that he "repeated the words that follows it, which was beyond the comprehension of anybody there."

Mr. Grinnell thus describes the prisoner on the witness stand:

> "Bram was of average height, and had a habit of standing erect with his shoulders thrown back. He was very alert. His naturally dark complexion was darkened by exposure. When his face was quiet it had a solid, business look—quite calculating. But when he spoke, a strange mixture of qualities was disclosed. His voice was resounding. Everyone could hear him everywhere. When speaking to a friend, his black eyes would shine and sparkle, he would show his white teeth under his

thick lips, and would put his hand in a persuasive manner on the person to whom he was talking. But when he was under cross-examination, his eyes became steadily fixed and hard to a startling degree, his mouth grew confidently firm, and he carried his head in a way that brought into prominence a very long under jaw. His manner when questioned about the murders was that of doing a piece of business that he must attend to very carefully and which was wearying everybody except himself. He testified with the air of quite willingly delivering a lecture upon a subject about which no one knew anything except himself, and he knew everything. He was very patient with his hearers and was effusively apologetic to his cross-examiner. His nerve, coolness, and power of endurance, made him apparently the freshest man in the court-room at the end of day after day. And his presence and conciliatory habit were so effective that many spectators who believed him guilty were sure that twelve nen would not find such a smooth talker guilty of such a crime as murder. But there were times during that long trial when more than one observer thought his expression remorseless."

The witnesses for the Government were, of course, introduced one at a time, and were excluded from court except when they were testifying. The prisoner had the advantage of hearing them all, and giving his explanation or making his denial of damaging statements. Often his explanation was plausible; sometimes it was

*From a sketch in "The Boston Post"*

Bram in Court at the Second Trial

not. He did not hear Mrs. Nash's scream, for instance, although her window and door were open, and the cry had been loud enough to wake Mr. Monks. The alternative theory to Bram's guilt, the theory of the defence, was that Charley Brown, seized by an attack of homicidal mania, had lashed the wheel—there were ropes for that purpose—descended into the cabin, taken down the axe, gone from one sleeping person to another in the semi-darkness, killed all three of them, gone up on deck again, put down the axe, and returned to the wheel,—all of this without being noticed by Bram who was on deck, and in charge of the ship. The only exception was Bram's statement that he saw Charley for a moment at the mizzen peak jig.

That evil spirit which protected the mysterious outside murderer of the Bordens must have been taking care of Charley Brown! Many mariners contended, and will contend, that to lash the wheel of a vessel of this kind, sailing eight knots in a fresh breeze, with a moderate sea running, would have been impossible for more than a minute. She would have fallen off, or else come up into the wind with her sails flapping, so as to rouse everybody on board.

Nothing more delighted, or exasperated, sea-faring folk and others who followed the case than the testimony on this question. As the long procession of old sea-captains, and other experts filed across the witness-stand, every sailor in New England, professional and amateur, took up the argument with vehemence. Wharves, forecastles, sailors' retreats, yachting clubs, resounded with the discussion. The defence produced nine ancient mariners of varied experience who swore that in their opinion the wheel might have been lashed for ten or even twenty minutes. Mr. Hoar, the attorney for the United States, must often have heard his University glee club sing that sea-ballad: "A capital ship for an ocean trip, was 'The Walloping Window-blind.'" I wonder if some of its lines did not recur to him:

The man at the wheel was taught to feel
  Contempt for the wildest blow,
And it often appeared, when the weather had cleared,
  That he'd been in his bunk below.

The Government was not permitted to rebut this evidence. But—to anticipate a little—at the second trial, the Government was allowed to produce their witnesses, and among others appeared a brother of the murdered Captain of the *Herbert Fuller*, who had succeeded to the command of that vessel. He stated as his belief, after one or two long voyages in the *Fuller*, that if the wheel were lashed under those conditions, she would come up and her sails begin to flap within two minutes. There is a legend, much enjoyed in my native city, that one of the fine old sea-dogs of that port expressed himself vigorously, even sulphurously, in the court, as to the duties of an officer of the deck toward a helmsman who deserted the wheel. I have read therefore with great interest, the testimony of Captain Benjamin Emerton, who was seventy-six years old, had been at sea for fifty-two years, had sailed in a barkentine, and about every other kind of vessel, and crossed the equator perhaps fifty times. But, although I have no doubt he spoke with animation, there is no record of sultry language. To the question:

"In case the man at the wheel leaves the wheel without orders, what is the duty of the officer in charge of the watch?" Captain Emerton's reply was merely: "Knock him down, or something else."

Expert testimony was introduced upon the subject of Charley Brown's sanity. Medical gentlemen, after listening to hypothetical questions describing Charley's behavior in Rotterdam and on the ship, gave it as their serious judgment that he was insane; other medical gentlemen, after hearing the same questions, said that he was not insane. There was much testimony about certain loose leaves from the log-book of the *Fuller* written up by Mate Bram. It was suggested that he tore out the original leaves, and wrote garbled accounts of the voyage in the book itself. One of the justices referred to this as "making something to be used as evidence, a pure manufacture at this time,"—language which he avoided at the second trial.

The case was given to the jury on New Year's Day, 1897. They returned to the court-room once to ask a question about the testimony, and again, later in the evening, to inform the justices that they saw no hope of reaching an agreement before the next morning. On the following morning, having again repeated that they had not agreed, Mr. Justice Colt read to them the statement of a judge about the desirability of reaching a verdict, if it were possible. They retired again, but again returned, to ask for information, which was denied. Finally, in the afternoon of January 2, after being out for more than twenty-six hours, and taking, it is said, fifty ballots, they brought in the verdict of "Guilty."

A motion for a new trial was argued during the same month, and before the justices who tried the case. It was denied. Mr. Justice Colt said: "We do not see how any intelligent, conscientious and painstaking jury, having listened to the whole trial and having seen the various witnesses, could have reached any different verdict." On March 9 Bram was brought before the court, for sentence. To the question if he had anything to say, he declared his innocence of the crime. He was sentenced, in these words:

"All things having been fully heard and understood by the Court, it is ordered that the verdict of the jury be confirmed, and that you, Thomas M. Bram, be taken back to the place from whence you came and there remain in close confinement until Friday, the eighteenth day of June, in the year of our Lord one thousand eight hundred and ninety-seven, and on that day, between the hours of eleven in the forenoon and two o'clock in the afternoon, you, the said Thomas M. Bram, be taken thence to the place of execution and that you there be hanged by the neck until you are dead.

"And may God, of His infinite goodness, have mercy on your soul."

The prisoner's only hope now lay in the Supreme Court of the United States. Exceptions under a writ of error were laid before that Court, and argued by Mr. French, of counsel for the defence, at the October term. The execution of the sentence was, of course, stayed by this fact. And the sailors of the *Herbert Fuller* had to remain in jail. The chief points relied upon in the argument were the admission of the testimony of the Halifax detective, Power; the questions which had been put by the Government to the sailors on the *Fuller* about the way in which she answered to the wheel; Justice Webb's remark about Bram's "manufacture" of the evidence; and the testimony of a medical witness, Dr. Draper, as to the possibility of a person standing over Captain Nash, and striking him with an axe, yet escaping blood-stains on his clothing. The witness had said that he would not necessarily be spattered with blood. The defence also contended that Bram should have been allowed to rebut the testimony as to his statement about residence in Nova Scotia, by exhibiting letters which he said he had shown to Captain Nash. He claimed that he had not deceived the Captain on that point.

The Supreme Court reversed the judgment of the first trial, set the verdict aside, and ordered a new trial. This they did because of the admission of Power's testimony. It was held that Bram's conversation with the detective was not a voluntary confession, and therefore was not admissible. The decision was not unanimous; Mr. Justice Brewer, Chief Justice Fuller, and Mr. Justice Brown dissented.

The second trial began March 16, 1898 and continued until April 20,—during a time of excitement because of the approach of the war against Spain. The new District Attorney for the United States, Boyd B. Jones, Esq., assisted by John H. Casey, Esq., appeared for the Government, and the prisoner was again represented by Messrs. Cotter and French. The trial took much longer than before, and was more extensive in almost every respect. The same judges were on the bench. Mr. Power of Halifax did not appear, but a new and important witness made appearance in the *Herbert Fuller*, herself, which the Government had brought to Boston for the trial. There had been much contention, official and unofficial, about the window in the after house, and whether Brown could have seen through it, into the dimly lighted chart-room, and in spite of the iron rods or guards which protected the glass. The jury in this trial visited the barkentine, and made their own experiments in looking through this window. Evidently they were not led, thereby, into doubt of Charley Brown's story.

Between the two trials something had happened which was to have a curious effect upon the fortunes of the accused man. By an Act of Congress, passed only a few days after the close of the first trial, it had been provided that in Federal courts, trying a charge of murder, juries were permitted, if they found the accused guilty, to qualify their verdict by adding the words "without capital punishment." This jury was instructed of the permissive clause in the law at the opening of the trial. They were out for ten hours and forty-five minutes, and found the prisoner "Guilty, without capital punishment."

Since Bram, if guilty, had committed three of the most abominable and inexcusable murders which can be imagined, what did this verdict mean? Had some of the jury changed their attitude since they were sworn, and discovered scruples against capital punishment? Or did this represent a compromise,—the only method of securing a verdict from some of the jurors? Had the new law saved the prisoner's neck? Or had it worked to his disadvantage, and changed what might have been a disagreement into a verdict? The newspapers reported that the outcome was looked upon as a compromise; that at both trials a majority of the jury had favored a verdict of guilty from the beginning of their deliberations; and that at the second trial, doubtful members had been won over to this verdict, though they were not sufficiently convinced to vote for what would result in a death sentence. The papers also said that the theory of Charley Brown's homicidal mania was evidently not accepted, and that both juries believed that he had looked through the window and witnessed the act to which he testified.

On the 12th of July, 1898, almost exactly two years after the murders, Bram was sentenced to imprisonment for life, and taken to the United States Penitentiary at Atlanta. He was released on parole August 27, 1913. After twice being found guilty of three atrocious murders, he thus served a little over five years for each of them. He was on parole for five years and seven months and during this time, says the Department of Justice, "he made a remarkable record for good conduct, being diligent in business, energetic, and law-abiding." Consequently, on April 22, 1919, President Wilson, who was then in Paris, granted him a full pardon. The notification of it was apparently delayed, but on June 18, 1919, the *Boston Evening Transcript* reported that Bram's lawyer, Mr. Cotter, had that day received a letter from him. It is characteristic of his epistolary style:

My dear and honorable lawyer:

It gives me indescribable pleasure to inform you that President has this day granted a full and unconditional pardon to your innocent client.

This is the closing chapter of a wonderful case.

I am gratefully and respectfully your humble servant

THOMAS M. C. BRAM.

I have been informed that Mr. Bram dwells, not without some prosperity, and certainly (if his portrait is a witness) not unhappily, in Atlanta, engaged in the wholesale peanut business.

The Bram case was probably the next most notorious in any court in Massachusetts, following the Borden trial. The two seem hardly comparable at first thought; there is a wide difference between the house on Second Street, in the glaring sunlight of an August noonday, and the gloomy cabin of the *Herbert Fuller*. The crime for which Bram was punished was a nocturne, a sea-piece, with a vague suggestion of piracy, and more than a slight odor of strong drink. This is far removed from the respectable atmosphere of the Central Congregational Church of Fall River. Yet there are some curious resemblances between the two murders. In each was a man and his wife most furiously attacked and slain, one of them asleep at the time, by somebody wielding an axe or hatchet. In each, was it impossible to produce the weapon in court. In each, the absence of blood stains on the clothing of the accused person was a strong point for the defence. In each, the defence urged that the murders seemed like the work of a maniac. In each, an unsuccessful effort was made to prove an earlier attempt to commit a crime, and the suggestion that poison was to be the weapon was in both cases. And in each the religious activities of the defendant were notable.

There is no doubt whatever that the Bram case has figured in fiction. Not, unfortunately, by the pen of Mr. James B. Connolly, who might have handled it, but in a story called "The After House," by Mrs. Mary Roberts Rinehart. It is a rather confused and jerky novel about a triple murder on a private yacht. The incidents, from about the middle of the story, follow some of the events on the *Herbert Fuller*. The Captain, a passenger, and a lady's maid are killed with an axe. Everyone suspects everyone else; the bodies are placed in a boat, which is finally towed astern. The mate is put on trial, but the jury disagrees, and, at last, guilt is fixed upon the helmsman, "Charley Jones," a homicidal maniac. What might have been a masterpiece of grim horror is dissipated into a second-rate tale about wealthy and fashionable folk, partly by this very mistake of setting.

The *Herbert Fuller* went to sea again, but she was a lady with a past, and found it wise, after a time, to change her name. A ship is never masculine, even if she is called the *Hercules*, but the *Fuller* took a feminine title, and it was as the *Margaret B. Rouss* that she sailed the ocean for nearly twenty years. Murder did not stalk through her cabin, nor piracy form any plots against her safety—for a while. But both were lying in wait for her, and in the name of what was said to be the most cultivated nation on earth, they put an end to her forever. On May 29, 1917, her Captain, Frederick L. Foote, and seven of her crew arrived without their ship, at "an American port," the war-time name for New York. They had sailed from St. Andrew's Bay, Florida, on February 4, for Genoa, with a cargo of pitch-pine. In April, while they were in mid-ocean, and probably unaware of it, America declared the war which Germany had been waging against her for two years. It need not have interested Captain Foote and his men; the sea was as deep and as cold for those non-combatants who were thrown into it by Germany's peaceful ministrations, as for those whom she drowned as an act of war. Hitherto, the killing of Americans, and the destruction of American property were pleasantries of the only nation which is privileged to be ruthless in war, and fraudulent in peace. And now, due to no solicitude of the enemy, Captain Foote and his men were home again, and saved alive after the destruction of the old *Herbert Fuller*.

Late in the afternoon of April 27, when off the coast of Monaco, the barkentine had been struck by a torpedo on the starboard side, amidships. The attack was made in characteristic fashion, on a harmless, unarmed merchant-vessel, carrying lumber. The torpedo, for all the Germans cared, might have blown to atoms everyone on board. It happened not to do so. It tore the planks open and let the sea pour into the hold. The crew launched the life-boat, and got into it. Everything seeming to be safe, the helpless ship fatally wounded, and no chance being apparent that it might commit sacrilege and defend itself, the submarine cautiously rose to the surface half a mile away, and looked at its victim. A boat put off, with a junior officer and four seamen, pulled over to the *Fuller*, which did not sink rapidly because of the lumber. After ordering Captain Foote to stand by with his boat, the officer and his party went on board the barkentine, where they spent two hours ransacking the cabin and staterooms, and filling their boat with all kinds of loot. One of their brotherhood had been there before them, if they had known it.

Then they came alongside the life-boat, and picked the men's pockets of money, tobacco, pipes, and food. They took sextant, compass, charts and chronometer. Truly, Blackbeard would have spat upon them. At last they allowed the Americans to depart. Captain Foote and his crew rowed forty-five miles—the sea was luckily smooth—to port, and climbed up to Monte Carlo. The Prince of Monaco and James Gordon Bennett took care of them, and sent them home.

As they rowed away, the Germans went back to the *Herbert Fuller*. They put bombs in the hold, blew her up, and watched her hull sink into the Mediterranean.

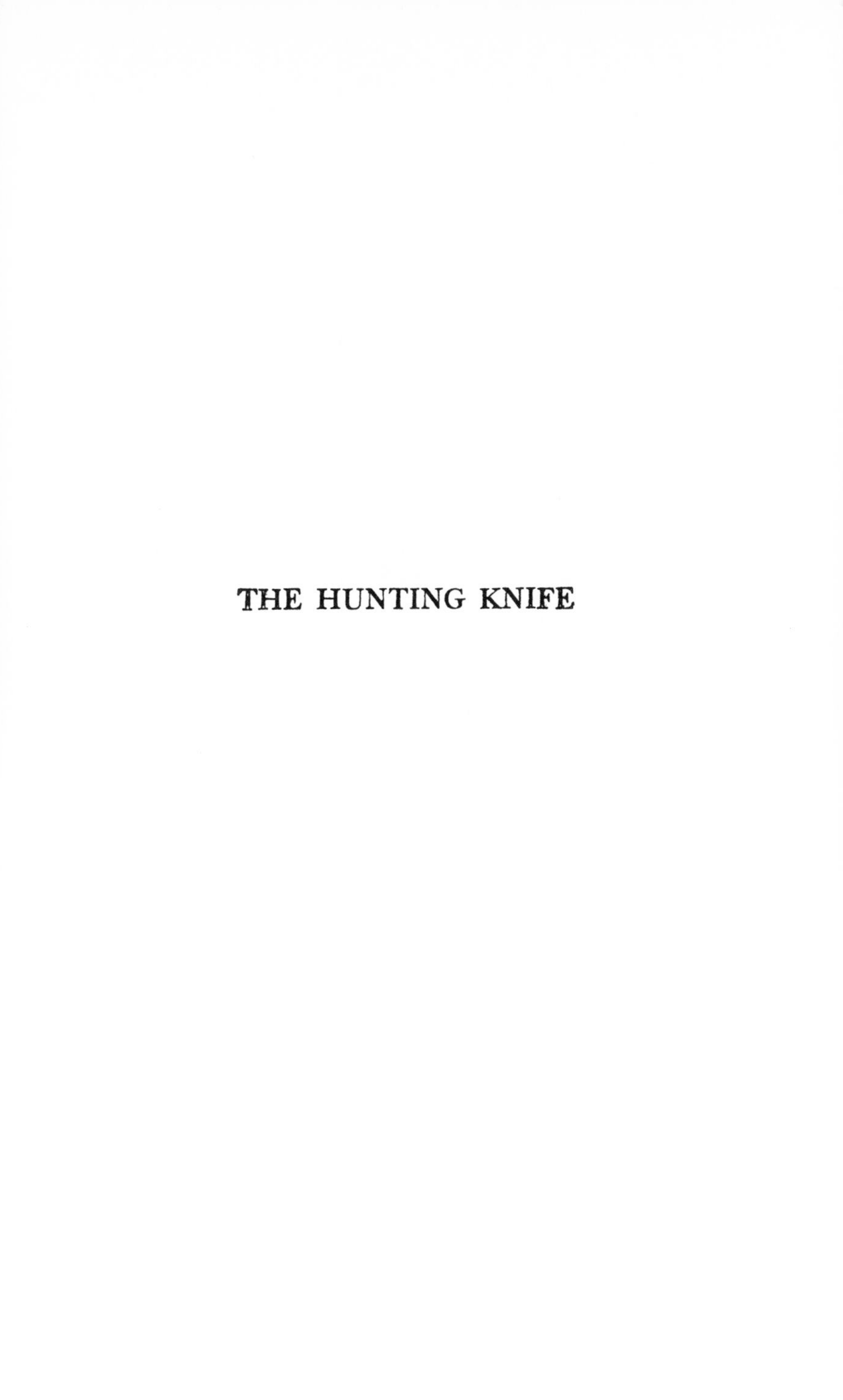

# THE HUNTING KNIFE

# THE HUNTING KNIFE

*This . . . stopped the further growth of one thing—the petition to the Governor for Injun Joe's pardon. The petition had been largely signed; many tearful and eloquent meetings had been held, and a committee of sappy women been appointed to go in deep mourning and wail around the Governor, and implore him to be a merciful ass and trample his duty under foot. Injun Joe was believed to have killed five citizens of the village, but what of that? If he had been Satan himself there would have been plenty of weaklings ready to scribble their names to a pardon petition. . . .*

—*The Adventures of Tom Sawyer.*

TWENTY years or more ago, if you walked due west from Cambridge, you might come, after four or five hours' stroll along pleasant country roads, to the delightful village of South Sudbury. Here you could rest and dine at the *Red Horse*, preserved and renamed, in honor of Longfellow, *The Wayside Inn.* Everything in the region was quiet and spacious, so far removed from the Nineteenth Century, so like the Eighteenth, that you would not have been surprised at the appearance of Earl Percy and his red-coats, or of any of those lean minutemen, with their flint-locks and powder-horns, who gave Percy such an uncomfortable time of it one warm April day on a neighboring road. The walk was through the streets of little towns, or through lanes bordered with willows, and flanked by open fields, meadows and low rolling hills. The Inn was unbelievably quiet and mellow; perhaps the most satisfactory thing of its kind in America.

Today, if you try that walk, you will be suffocated by gasoline fumes, or have your bruised form hurled into the nearest ditch by one of the motor-cars which have chased pedestrians off the highways. *The Wayside Inn* is owned by the king of all the automobile makers; and this is well, since he has saved it from destruction. But there is little pleasure in looking at the corpulent motorists who swarm upon the country roads.

Between Cambridge and Sudbury, the rule seemed to be that the names of all towns should begin with W. There was Watertown, Waltham, Weston, and Wayland. The reason for Waltham's celebrity is known to everybody; if Wayland is famous I do not know why, and only remember it as the subject of a pretty set of verses in "Songs from Vagabondia." Weston, exactly twenty years ago, had an undesirable celebrity for a little while; one which was probably all the more resented by the citizens since it was due to the atrocious action of a resident of another town.

On the last day of March, 1904, there lived on South Avenue, Weston, a family named Page. The house had been their summer home for over twenty years; they dwelt in Boston during the cold weather. For the past five or six years however, they had lived in Weston all the year, only one member of the family going daily into the city. Mr. Edward Page had retired from business; he was about seventy-eight years old. His wife had died nearly two years earlier. His son Harold, a clerk in the freight office of the Boston and Albany Railroad, in the South Station, took a train for Boston about eight every morning. He was fond of shooting and fishing; he bred and kept a few dogs, and sometimes sold one of them. His sister, Miss Mabel Page, a woman about forty-one years old, and the housekeeper, Amy Roberts, made up the rest of the family.

March 31st was one of the deceptive days of early spring, beginning with such promise as to lure walkers into the country roads; growing colder and more threatening as the afternoon came on; and finally ending in a return to winter. Mr. Harold Page departed for the city at the usual time. His father set out on a ramble at about half-past nine. The house-keeper, an hour later, went away for the day. Miss Page gave her money for her expenses, and for some shopping. Miss Roberts observed that she returned a ten dollar bill, and one or two others, to a purse, which she replaced in the drawer of a table. Then the housekeeper went on her way by the street-car to Watertown; to Cambridge, where she consulted her physician; and finally into Boston for her shopping. Before eleven o'clock Miss Page was left alone in the house; this, perhaps, was not a frequent occurrence, but it would have caused her no uneasiness. The house was in sight of others; the neighborhood was quiet and peaceful.

The elder Mr. Page went to the post-office at Auburndale; there is little or no division between the towns and villages in this region. A neighbor's coachman had been sent to drive him over to Auburndale, and after his arrival there he waited a few minutes for the opening of the public library, at ten o'clock. He had intended to go in town, but abandoned the idea on reading in the morning paper that a storm was predicted. He read until noon, when the library closed for two or three hours. He walked toward Waltham, called at a friend's house, and then made his way back to Auburndale, where he inspected a stable recently built by another of his friends. The coachman's wife opened the stable and showed him about in it. Then he returned, walking slowly, and resting from time to time, to his own home in Weston. He arrived there at about two o'clock.

The pleasant spring morning had attracted more than one other rambler into those roads and lanes. One of them was a resident of Auburndale, a young man named Charles Louis Tucker. He was a widower of twenty-four; his wife had died a trifle less than a year earlier. He had been in various occupations,—working for one of the men who let boats at Riverside, where everybody goes for boating or canoeing on the Charles; in the South Station, as baggage clerk and elevator boy; and recently at Thorp and Martin's, the Boston stationers. He had seen and known Mr. Harold Page for six years, but the acquaintance was slight; Mr. Page knew only his last name. On two occasions he had been at the Page house for a few moments. In 1902, he called one Sunday, talked with Mr. Page and his sister, entered the house for a while, visited the barn and bought a dog. On this day in March, 1904, however, Mr. Tucker was not in employment; his were idle hands.

He was regarded by some of his acquaintances as a harmless young man, and it was in token of this, perhaps, that they called him "Tommy Tucker." While the elder Mr. Page was wandering about Auburndale and Weston, Mr. Tucker also went for a stroll. According to a description of it which he gave later, it was an excursion both idyllic and innocent; by another version, which he found it wise to impart to a selected few, it was still idyllic, but not precisely innocent; a third and harsher description of his perambulations, never assented to by Mr. Tucker, denied it either of these qualities. At any rate, he said that he spent the morning dutifully working on the lawn of his parents' house. At noon, he changed his clothes and ate his mid-day meal. Then he walked down to the bridge at Weston; he named some persons who saw him. He walked up to South Avenue; at one place he saw a man digging in a trench. Everybody—Amy Roberts, Mr. Tucker, and everyone else—saw this man in the trench and remembered him, and it is not to be wondered at, for he bore an illustrious name: Mr. Dooley. Tucker loitered at one place to watch a squirrel—a winsome incident—and returned to his home about one o'clock.

He did not go in, as he met a friend, one Bourne. Together they walked down to Weston bridge again. Here they met a youth named Arthur Woodward driving a fish-wagon. Woodward may not have interested them especially, nor his fish, but his companion did. She was named, so it appeared, Mabel Walker, and her home was in Damariscotta, Maine. She waved her handkerchief and, like Woodward, seemed disposed to sociability. The two young men accepted an invitation to drive for a while on the fish-wagon. Mr. Tucker sat on the seat, between Woodward and the young lady from Maine. Mr. Bourne clambered into the rear of the wagon,—amongst the fish. After a while the company of the driver, of Bourne, or the fish, began to pall upon the other two, and they dismounted, and went for a walk together. Then they went over to the athletic grounds to watch the trap-shooting.

Finally Tucker bade Miss Walker good-bye, and returned to his home. There was at least one incident in connection with this day which he did not mention. He had carried with him—rather unnecessarily, for a morning's walk in the vicinity—a hunting knife in a sheath,—a knife with a blade about five inches long.

A little after eleven a man named Maynard came to the Page house delivering laundry. He rang at the front door and left a package with Miss Page. No other person was seen to come. At about ten minutes after two, Mr. Edward Page returned. He went to the rear door and found it fastened; he came to the front, and that door, contrary to custom, was unlocked. He opened it and went in. Up to this point the incidents remind us, in some measure, of Mr. Borden's return to his home. Mr. Page went to the pantry and had something to eat: a slice of bread and a glass of cider. He sat down and ate at leisure, for perhaps ten or fifteen minutes. Then he returned to the front room, where he observed his daughter's work as she had left it: a dress, her sewing basket and thimble. The house was very quiet, and it struck the old man as unusual that he did not hear his daughter anywhere. He decided to go upstairs to look for her. At the head of the stairs he was surprised to find the two doors of Miss Page's room closed; ordinarily they were open in the day to light the staircase. He opened one of the doors and looked in. His daughter was lying on her back on the floor; the eyes were open and seemed to look at him. She was fully clothed except that she wore an underskirt, but no overskirt. She wore a hat and walking boots as if she had been about to go out.

Mr. Page felt his daughter's hand, and found it cold. He tried to listen to her heart-beat; he spoke to her, but she was dead. He saw blood on the floor, and looking at her throat saw a jagged wound in the neck. After a short time, he went down-stairs and looked about in the main living-room. He noticed that the fire in the open fire-place had gone out; had been put out, apparently, by the removal of the two logs so that they lay beside the andirons. On a table he found a small slip of paper, bearing a message in Miss Page's handwriting. This note is an odd and almost inexplicable feature; I do not recall a parallel instance in any other case of which I have read. It was as follows:

> Have just heard that Harold is hurt and at the Massachusetts Hospital. Have gone in 12 o'clock. Will leave key in front side door with barn key. Will telephone Mrs. Bennett.

Mr. Page went out to summon help, to ask the neighbors for assistance, to send for a doctor, and to learn what had happened to his son. By means of the nearest telephone, in Mrs. Bennett's home, he got into communication with the South Station in Boston, and asked about Harold Page. The answer was that the young man was there and would speak for himself. Nothing had happened to him; he had not been hurt. He was told, by his father, of his sister's death, and started for home. He went first to the home of a married sister who lived in town, and left word of the death with her.

A doctor came during the afternoon, and another, the Medical Examiner, at about six o'clock. By that time it was not only dark but stormy, a snow-storm. The doctors viewed the body by the uncertain light of hand-lamps, and to them the wound in the throat seemed to resemble the awkward gash often made by suicides. They talked with the family, but were unable to come to any decision. The Medical Examiner left a note for the undertaker, telling him not to embalm the body until a further examination had been held. When the undertaker came, at midnight, he found two other wounds: one in the chest and one in the back. The latter wound, together with the absence of a weapon, disposed of any theory of suicide. The Medical Examiner was sent for again, and the police were notified that this was a murder. Death had been caused by the wound in the chest which had penetrated the heart. This, and the wound in the throat, were each of a depth of five inches. The over-skirt of the dead woman was found on the floor near the body. The hooks which held the waist had been pulled out, and red fibers of a straw carpet were found embedded in the skirt. As there were no red fibers in the carpet in the bed-room, where her body was found, and as there were in the carpet in the hall outside, and in the room downstairs, it was apparent that the murder had occurred elsewhere, and that the body had been dragged into the bedroom. Another curious bit of writing was found in the house; in the room with the body. It was placed on the floor, and seemed to have been deliberately placed to attract attention. It bore, in pencil, the words: "J. L. Morton, Charlestown, Mass." It was written in a back hand, some of the letters started one way, and then started again, and written over. The handwriting was not that of anybody in the family. From the purse in the room downstairs, the purse in which the housekeeper had seen twelve or more dollars in bills that morning, all the money, except for some change, was missing.

The newspapers were rather impatient with the police for not making an immediate arrest. The murder was so brutal, so unexplainable and unusual, that it caused a great sensation. All who had been in the neighborhood were questioned, and the accuracy of their statements investigated. Four days after the murder, Tucker, merely as a person known to have been nearby, was asked for an interview by the police. He told them the story of his walk, of his work and his amusements on that day, practically as it has been related here. He was not put under arrest; there was no direct cause for suspicion against him. At the end of the interview, he was permitted to go home. But the papers printed the fact that he had been at the police-station, and published his picture. This, in *The Boston Post*, fell into the hands of young Woodward, the driver of the fish-wagon, and thereby served the cause of justice. Woodward disclosed to his father a certain fact, and showed him an interesting object. It was the leather sheath for a knife. He had found it on the seat of the wagon, a few moments after Tucker had left him on March 31. On finding it, Woodward put it into his pocket and took it home; it carried no suggestion for him until, five days later, he read of Tucker's association with the crime. The sheath was for a knife about five inches in length; there were the marks of teeth in one corner of it. The elder Woodward notified the police of Weston, and handed over the sheath to them.

It had been a portentous moment for Mr. Tucker when Mabel Walker waved her handkerchief, and he accepted the invitation; the incident seemed trifling, but its effect was not. Of another trifling incident in an imaginary mystery, its inventor wrote: "Among the mighty store of wonderful chains that are forever forging, day and night, in the vast iron-works of time and circumstance, there was one chain forged in the moment of that small conclusion, riveted to the foundations of heaven and earth, and gifted with invincible force to hold and drag." There is a story of a lady who dreamed one night that a hearse drove up to her door, and that the driver, a hideous looking man, with fiery red hair, and two front teeth missing, beckoned her to come. She woke in deadly terror, and could with difficulty get to sleep again that night. On the following day she was on one of the upper floors of a tall office-building waiting for the lift. When it arrived and its door was opened, she saw, to her horror, that the man running it was the same ugly creature with the red hair, beckoning her in with the gesture he had used in the nightmare. She drew back, and refused to step inside. The lift started without her; fell to the bottom of the shaft, and killed most of the occupants. But nothing had warned Tucker that, for him, young Woodward was Jack Ketch himself; and that his wagon might have been the cart which used to rattle up to Tyburn.

Tucker was taken again to a police-station and given the usual warning of his right to answer questions or not as he chose, and of his risk, if he spoke, of having his words used against him. He was asked if he owned the sheath of a knife, and he denied that he did. An officer who was examining one of his overcoats, then held up this sheath, and asked if it were his. He then admitted it, and said that on the third day after the murder, fearing that he was suspected, he had taken the sheath from a drawer in his room, and put it into the overcoat pocket to conceal it from the police. (This was the sheath, which, all the time since the day of the murder, had been in Woodward's possession.) He denied that he had ever owned a hunting knife, except one which he had sold a year before, and one which he had lost in the river two years earlier. He permitted a dentist to take a cast of his teeth, and it was found to correspond with the marks of teeth on the sheath. During this examination his house was searched. In the pocket of a coat in his room, were found three fragments of a knife-blade; the handle was missing. The blade had been broken, twisted, and filed. But it was found to be a blade originally about five inches in length; it bore blood-stains. In the pocket with it was a pin with a Canadian emblem, afterwards declared by Amy Roberts to be Miss Page's property. Tucker was shown the broken knife-blade, and he now admitted that it belonged to him, and said that he tried to destroy it when he became aware that he was suspected by the police. At the end of the questions he was placed under arrest.

Now that somebody was actually held for the murder a few of the newspapers found him an object of sympathy. They expressed doubts of his guilt. He became "the boy, Tucker," an unfortunate youth undergoing persecution by the police. This phrase, "the boy," became so popular, was so often repeated, and seemed so effective in winning him friends and sympathizers, that the experiment was presently tried of applying it to another man who was held for murder a few months afterwards. But it was abandoned, when the discovery was made that this male child was forty-eight years old.

It is not effective, except to people totally ignorant about crime and criminals, to argue that a man accused of murder cannot be guilty because he is only twenty, twenty-two or twenty-four years old. An astonishing number of tender-hearted persons retain a touching faith in their ability to read the character by a glance at a portrait. "Why, he doesn't look like a criminal!" they exclaim, and are instantly ready to sign a petition in his behalf. It does not occur to them that if murderers and thieves looked their parts, there would be little crime, since nobody would risk life or property with them. The work of the police would be simple; they would merely have to go about arresting folk who look like "criminals." Not long ago there were living in an Eastern city two men with the same surname; one was a notorious gambler and the other an officer of a university. The university man wore clothes of a loud pattern and sporting cut; his face suggested that he spent his days and nights dealing faro, or running a roulette wheel. But the gambler, in dress and appearance, might have been a rather austere churchman,—a dean or an archdeacon. Sherlock Holmes told Watson that the most villainous looking man of his acquaintance was a philanthropist who had spent half a million on the London poor, while the most charming woman he had ever seen poisoned her husband and three children for their insurance money.

More than nine months after the murder, on January 2, 1905, Tucker was put on trial before the Superior Court, at East Cambridge. The Court consisted of Justices Edgar J. Sherman and Henry N. Sheldon. The case was prosecuted for the Commonwealth by the Attorney General, Herbert Parker, Esq., the District Attorney, George A. Sanderson, Esq., and his assistant, Hugh Bancroft, Esq. For the prisoner appeared James H. Vahey, Esq., Thomas F. Vahey, Esq., and Charles H. Innes, Esq.

The case depended entirely upon circumstantial evidence. Nobody had seen Tucker enter or leave the Page house. The Government sought to prove that he had the opportunity to commit the murder; that he was in the vicinity. That he had the motive of theft, and that this was proved by his possession not only of the "Canadian pin," but of a ten dollar bill and other money which he had shortly after the crime, although he was known to be without money before the crime. Allusions were made to the possibility of a further motive, but no evidence was introduced charging the attempt or commission of any crime other than murder and robbery. That his knife fitted the wounds and the tears in the clothing of the dead woman, and that he had attempted to destroy evidence by breaking this knife. That he had told lies about his whereabouts at the time of the murder, and about his possession of the knife, sheath, and pin. And that the "J. L. Morton" note was in his handwriting, and had been left in the house to divert suspicion. They produced a witness named J. D. Morton, who worked, as Tucker had formerly done, in the South Station. The inference was that the similar name was one which might have occurred to him, or possibly that he might have presented himself at the house under that name. The latter was not urged, and seems improbable, since Miss Page had seen him at least once, and had heard his real name.

The defence contested all these assertions of the Government. They produced witnesses to try to corroborate the prisoner's statements about his walk on March 31; to prove that the pin was his own, that they had seen him wearing it in his cap before the murder; and to break down other points made by the prosecution.

Some of these witnesses were evidently partisan, some appeared to be perjured, and their general effect was not advantageous to the prisoner. Judge Sherman commented afterwards that the defence would have done better to rest on the Government's case. Yet Tucker's cause was presented with ingenuity and the utmost persistence; no technicality known to the law was neglected in his behalf, and no evidence introduced against him without a contest, if there was the least opportunity for one.

One of the principal struggles centered around the Morton note, and the question of hand-writing. The Government produced numerous samples of Tucker's writing, from one of the firms where he had been employed. There was also a curious post-card, found in his pocket, on which he had written various names and words, including "Morton" and "Charlestown." Surely the psycho-analysts could have made something of this, had they been present to darken counsel. In their place, there appeared hand-writing experts, who waged a tremendous battle. The jury listened for hours to testimony about "the axis of the Capital C" and "the upper lobe of the L." They might have fainted beneath the strain had not the proceedings been lightened, on one day, by the cross-examination of a famous expert, in which the Attorney General and the witness outdid Lord Chesterfield in courtly consideration for each other. I am not sure that it is known what view the jury finally took of the authorship of the Morton note, but even without it, the Government's case was very strong.

The other note which, it is undisputed, was written by Miss Page, herself, probably only a few minutes before her death, the one beginning "Have just heard that Harold is hurt," opens a field for speculation. It is, in a grim sense, full of fascination when we consider that it represents a rare and extraordinary situation: the interview of a murderer with his victim, while the latter is still unaware of danger. Such a scene appealed to the imagination of Stevenson, and he made use of it in the conversation between Markheim and the dealer in the lonely shop. In actual murders, what happens at such a time usually remains forever unknown; it did so in this case. Why did the slayer of Mabel Page leave this note behind him? Was it written while he waited outside, or in a passage, and did he overlook it, or was he unaware even of its existence? It might have named him! Did the fact that he told her this falsehood about her brother indicate an attempt to get her out of the house and away, so that he could plunder it at leisure? Did he know that the elder Mr. Page and Amy Roberts were both absent, and was this story concocted before he reached the house, to make the last member of the family leave it for him to rob? He could not have expected to be left there alone. The Government suggested that he may have offered to go with Miss Page to the hospital; that he stayed below while she went upstairs to put on her hat and walking-boots; that on coming down she found him rifling her purse; that she fled to call for help, and that the murder took place then to prevent his arrest for theft. Did he come there with the murder in mind, or come merely to steal?

There is one fact which suggests that he must have intended her death before he knocked at her door: he was known to her, and if he told her this lie about her brother, and then left her alive, how could he explain it afterwards?

The trial was fully reported, and followed with intense interest. One newspaper made preparations to announce the verdict if it were rendered at night, by electric signals, as if it were the result of a Presidential election. Judge Sherman wrote: "When the trial commenced I think the public feeling was perhaps that the prisoner was guilty, but the Government had not sufficient evidence to convict him . . . the newspapers, while professing to publish all the evidence, were only in fact publishing a small part of it with comments upon it unfavorable to the Government, so that nearly the whole New England public were of the opinion that there was not sufficient evidence to convict the prisoner. The prisoner, who was a young man, not bad looking, had much sympathy in his favor."

The Hearst newspapers, which a little later found in Harry Thaw a modern St. George, discovered in Tucker a person deserving their best efforts in his behalf. One of their head lines was "Kill Tucker! Cries Parker,"—and to the childish minds of the readers of Hearst newspapers it may have seemed that the only blood-guilty persons were the chief law officer of the Commonwealth and his assistants.

The prisoner did not testify in his own behalf; and comment will later be made upon this fact. Before the charge was given to the jury, he was permitted to address them. He did not have the good judgment to confine his remarks to thirteen words, but made a speech of two or three minutes' length. In it he said little of importance, except to deny his connection with the murder, to give a much expurgated account of his doings on March 31, to deny that he wrote the Morton note, to say that he broke up the knife because he was frightened when the police began coming to his house, and to describe himself on the day of the murder as "happy as any boy could be." Even he had adopted the popular phraseology, and twice referred to himself as a "boy."

On the twentieth day of the trial, January 24, the jury went out at about 2 P. M. They came in, during the evening, with two questions which foreshadowed the verdict: what constitutes malice aforethought, and whether they were obliged to specify the degree of murder in case of a verdict of guilty. Later in the evening they asked two more questions of the Court, and after going out again, returned in about fifteen minutes. Shortly after ten o'clock they gave in their verdict: "Guilty of murder in the first degree."

The motion for a new trial was made on the grounds that a juror took notes during the first trial; that erroneous instructions were given the jury as to what constitutes deliberately premeditated malice aforethought; and that the verdict was against the weight of the evidence. The same Court which had sat in the trial denied the motion, saying that "a verdict of acquittal would have been a failure of justice." The judges further expressed their belief that practically all the contentions of the Government had been established. They said that in their opinion the Morton note was written by Tucker in the Page house "for the purpose of misleading future inquiry, and this without giving weight to any of the expert testimony upon handwriting," that the "Canadian pin" was stolen by him from the house, and that much of the evidence produced at the trial on his behalf was untrue.

Exceptions were taken to the Supreme Judicial Court of the State, and over-ruled. Another motion for a new trial was filed, and over-ruled by Mr. Justice Sherman. An application for a writ of error was made to the Supreme Court of the United States; it was denied. Finally, on January 27, 1906, nearly two years after the murder, Judge Sherman, in a speech of considerable length, sentenced Tucker to suffer death during the week beginning June 10, "by the passage of electricity through [his] body."

But the most extraordinary part of the struggle to save this man had just begun. As the time for the execution of the sentence approached, far-reaching efforts were made, in an appeal to the Governor of Massachusetts to commute the sentence to life-imprisonment. The agitation grew to enormous proportions. Thousands of names were signed to petitions. The names of entire families, including in some instances, children in the cradle, were solemnly set down at the foot of these documents. The petitioners and the agitators in behalf of Tucker included every possible variety of citizen; they were actuated by every motive. There were his attorneys, acting, naturally enough, in his interest; there were some respectable and distinguished persons who were probably not familiar with the case or the evidence, but sincere in their belief that his guilt was doubtful; there were the opponents of capital punishment whose feelings suffer at the thought of the execution of the death sentence. As usual, the latter class were divided into those who honestly and sincerely oppose the death penalty as such; and those who disingenuously pretend to believe in the innocence of all convicted murderers, although their real intention is to prevent the enforcement of this law. There were concerned in the Tucker agitation persons who were simply actuated by political enmity to the State Government; and others of the kind who will always join in the effort to save any especially shocking or notorious murderer, but pay little attention to the fate of the obscure one. And finally there were a great number of the chuckle-headed folk, who would balk at contributing a one-cent postage-stamp to save a condemned man, but are willing to sign a petition about almost anything, if someone else provides the pen, ink, and paper.

Some of these groups, aided by the worst elements in journalism, produced a tumult almost unprecedented in the criminal history of the State.[1] They were willing

[1] Exceeded perhaps, in its worst phases, by the agitation about a peculiarly cold-blooded and undesirable person, named Mrs. Rogers, in Vermont, in 1905. Hysteria passed all bounds, in that instance, and in addition to the petitions, some of the stratagems proposed or attempted in her behalf suggest the atmosphere of the 18th century, and the chronicles of Newgate.

to attack and traduce any officer of the Commonwealth; persecute and vilify any witness whose testimony was unpalatable to them; pursue with slander the family of the dead woman; and generally to let the frame of things disjoint, if only they might preserve the life of a notoriously worthless man who was also guilty of an abominable murder. Tucker, in their descriptions, began to look fairly seraphic. And this in a community whose citizens are seldom accused of undue sentimentalism; whose faults are generally asserted to be those of intellectual coldness rather than of emotional excitement.

The Governor of Massachusetts, the late Curtis Guild, Jr., gave an extended hearing to the petitioners, on June 5. The prisoner was represented by his attorneys; the justices were present, while the State was represented by Messrs. Parker and Sanderson, and the new Attorney General, Mr. Malone. A dozen witnesses were heard, and both Mr. Parker and Mr. Vahey made arguments. The report of the hearing occupies over two hundred type-written sheets. Part of the testimony offered concerned the "Canadian pin"; part of it was an attempt at retraction of some medical testimony not essential to the Government's case; part was irresponsible gossip or hearsay about strange men seen in remote places, or possible weapons picked up in ditches. In two days, the Governor gave out a reply, nearly all of which is reprinted here. It is not only what Mr. Bram would call "the closing chapter of a wonderful case," but it forms one of the most conscientious and admirable replies ever made, to my knowledge, to a petition of the kind.

*To the Petitioners for the Commutation of the Sentence of Charles L. Tucker.*

I have given to your petition and to the case of Charles L. Tucker, convicted of the murder of Mabel Page, the most careful consideration. Some time since I began my own investigation of the case.

I have read all the evidence presented in the lower court and the official stenographic report (2,696 pages) of the proceedings in the Superior Court, together with various affidavits and reports submitted to me.

I have given a lengthy hearing to the counsel for the prisoner and to all witnesses as to fact whom they chose to summon, even when the testimony offered was such as could not be heard in a court of justice, recognizing that the Governor, on a plea of clemency, is not bound by technical laws of evidence. I have personally examined the neighborhood of the murder, and have on foot passed, with time tests, over the roads and ways about the Page house in Weston and at about the hour of the day when the murder was committed. I have examined all the various exhibits in the case, and have myself fitted the blade of the knife of Charles L. Tucker into the slit in the blood-stained corset of Mabel Page.

I have no right, remembering my oath to enforce the laws of this Commonwealth, to consider my own or other men's opinions of the character of those laws, or to stay the execution of any law because of my opinion or of any other man's opinion. I have no right to refuse to enforce the law in regard to capital punishment, on the ground that that law is abhorrent to any person or persons.

In considering so serious a case all prejudice should be removed and evidence carefully sifted. Irresponsible talk in regard to the manner in which the prisoner's wife met her death in his company can be given no more consideration than similar irresponsible talk of unidentified persons in Connecticut who looked as if they might have committed some crime somewhere.

[The Governor then reviewed all the steps in legal procedure in the case, after which he continued, as follows:]

Accordingly, at the hearing before me, at the Executive Chamber, Justices Sheldon and Sherman, who occupied the bench during the trial, were present at my invitation. They have reported as follows on the evidence offered:

*To His Excellency the Governor.*

After carefully considering the testimony to which we listened yesterday, we respectfully report as follows:

A large part of this evidence was the merest hearsay, and could not have been considered in court. Much of this and also of the other evidence was only conjectural. The comparatively small portion that could have any legitimate bearing was cumulative, and not of a character that seemed to us to command confidence, or to warrant any expectation that if produced at the trial it properly could have brought about a different result from that which was reached. We cannot find that there would now be any material change in the testimony of the medical experts. We heard nothing to meet the strong evidence of guilt which was offered at the trial.

Accordingly, if this were a question of setting aside the verdict of the jury, we should be unable to do so.

Very respectfully, your obedient servants,

EDGAR J. SHERMAN,
HENRY N. SHELDON.

Boston, June 6, 1906.

This important report commands serious consideration.

The attempt at the hearing before me to offer a literary parody as evidence against the law officers of the Commonwealth but emphasizes their faithful, fair and intelligent services.

No medical authority who actually himself saw the wounds on the body of Mabel Page has ever wavered in his statement that they might have been made by a knife of the exact measurement of that which Tucker had tried to destroy, but which was found in fragments before he had time to dispose of them, in the side pocket of his coat, in company with a stick pin sworn to have belonged to his victim. Men do not habitually carry stick pins loose in the side pockets of their coats. If this were one of the various pins that really did belong to Tucker, it is extraordinary that it should have been found in such an unusual place, in company with fragments of a knife which he confessed he was trying to destroy because they might be used to incriminate him. Why, regardless of ownership, was he trying to hide that pin?

A discussion of all the numerous points of evidence incriminating the prisoner is unnecessary; they are a matter of record.

Every decision handed down by every judicial authority to whom disputed questions of law have been referred has affirmed the correctness of the rulings in this case. Not only did every member of that jury, to whom the original evidence, ungarbled and undistorted, was presented, find the prisoner guilty, but the judge who pronounced sentence upon him, after every possible appeal to the judiciary had been exhausted, declared the verdict of murder in the first degree "proper, lawful and just." He even added: "It is hard to imagine a more wanton, wicked and causeless murder than this, of a virtuous and blameless woman."

The causes usually urged for mercy to a convicted criminal are either extreme youth, notable public service, intense provocation or a previously blameless life. No such plea can be entered for the prisoner. He is not a boy. Men of no greater age than his at the time of the murder have served in national parliaments and commanded armies that have changed the destinies of the world. Not only is no claim of public service made for the prisoner, but he never rose or remained for any great length of time in any private employment. Neither Mabel Page nor any of her family had ever wronged him or his. His habits of life, as disclosed to me by investigation, through official and other sources, seem almost impossible to one whose bitter duty it is to resist the appeals of his clear-eyed brother, his sorrowing mother and his father, honored and respected of all men.

I must, however, remember that other home,—a pure and lovely girl murdered in a lonely house; a father martyred by sensationalism; a devoted sister driven to the verge of nervous prostration; and a faithful working girl persecuted by threats of bodily harm.

Proof of the miserable habit of life of this unhappy young man, as disclosed by incidents in connection with this trial, is confirmed by my own independent investigation.

The search warrant, prepared, though not used, against Tucker did not specify the knife used in the murder, but did specify certain goods stolen on other occasions by the prisoner, which were returned to their owners, chiefly by the prisoner, before his arrest.

The same plea, of having returned the fruits of a crime after its commission, has been publicly made to excuse the prisoner for an admitted forgery.

At the hearing before me the prisoner's counsel

asserted that the prisoner on the day of the murder "committed an offence with Mabel Walker." The evidence of the lower court, later confirmed by expert medical evidence summoned by both sides, furnishes uncontested proof that the prisoner was not accustomed to recognize even the bounds established by nature in the gratification of his passions.

In common with every other responsible person in this case, sworn to act in accordance with his convictions as to the prisoner's guilt or innocence, I am compelled to an undoubting belief in his guilt.

Neither, therefore, on the ground urged that the verdict was unwarranted by the evidence, nor on the grounds usually urged, can I interfere with the execution of this just sentence. Every citizen must sympathize and sorrow with this unhappy man's afflicted family; but of more importance than the life of any one citizen is the protection by government of the life of every citizen, is the safeguarding of women's chastity in the lonely farmhouse as well as in the patrolled streets of the city, is the assurance to the people that the ordered action of their courts is to be respected, and that irresponsible agitation cannot be substituted for law and order in this Commonwealth.

This melancholy chapter in our history may not have been written in vain if it serves to warn the youth of our Commonwealth, tempted by the allurements of vice to ignoble life, that the wages of sin is death; if it serves to show that government in Massachusetts still stands on the rock of her own

Constitution, to the end that it may be "A government of laws and not of men."

CURTIS GUILD, JR.

Executive Chambers, State House, Boston, June 7, 1906.

Only a few days remained before the time set for execution of the sentence, but the Tucker party continued its agitation. Their actions would have been less mysterious had the prisoner been a woman, had he enjoyed the support of any one sect or organization, or had the case against him depended upon any one point, such as the identity of the stolen pin. Much of their argument was concentrated upon the pin, as if a doubt about that should have upset the conviction. As the hubbub increased, and as some of the more reckless writers and speakers tried to blacken the character of everyone connected with the Government, brighter and more shining in their estimation grew the personality of Tucker. He was a martyred boy, a model for youth, a hero, a saint being hounded to his death by blood-thirsty men.

This naïve conception of a State Executive who refuses to "be a merciful ass and trample his duty under foot," as if *he* were the murderer, has been illustrated by the remark of a Mrs. Place, when she was awaiting her execution in Sing Sing, and heard that the Governor of New York, who had served in the Spanish War, had refused to interfere with her sentence:

"That soldier-man likes killing things, and he is going to kill me."

She glided gracefully over her own *penchant* for killing things: husbands, for instance.

Perhaps the notoriety and brutality of Tucker's crime started the efforts to save him. After that, the agitation grew by what it fed upon. A day or two before June 10 there was a meeting in his behalf in Faneuil Hall. Somebody sent a telegram to the President of the United States, alleging that he had the right to intervene under some Federal law, and urging him to do so. The President, Mr. Roosevelt, replied in a telegram to Governor Guild, saying that he knew of no legal sanction which would permit him to interfere in such a case. He added, characteristically, that even if he had such power he would not exercise it, as he considered that the Governor's refusal to interfere was entirely correct. Such expressions of opinion from that President often caused grief to many worthy persons; since his day some of them have been heard to lament that his outspoken manner is not more often imitated by other public men.

In the evening of June 11 a last appeal was made by a clergyman. The Governor listened to him for over an hour, but at the end declined to alter his decision. The prisoner, in a letter, written a few days before, to his attorney, had continued to protest his innocence. The sentence of death was executed a few minutes after midnight on June 12. The condemned man read a short statement which neither confessed guilt nor affirmed innocence. He had received baptism, and this statement was a religious declaration, asking for the pardon of his own sins, and granting forgiveness to his enemies.

After the execution there appeared in the papers a statement by Tucker's senior counsel, James H. Vahey, Esq., discussing his client's failure to take the witness stand. The substance of it was this:

> The failure of the defendant to testify has also been a subject of much comment and we feel that the public ought to know exactly what the reasons were for the defendant's failure to testify.
>
> This question gave us great concern throughout the trial and up to the moment when it was definitely determined that the prisoner would not testify. While the whole matter had remained in abeyance, I think we all had a feeling that the defendant would take the stand.
>
> The evidence in the case was concluded on Saturday, January 21. On Friday, January 20, all the evidence had practically been presented, except that of the defendant, if he were to testify, and the court had adjourned a little earlier that day in order that we might have some farther time to reflect on that subject. I do not know that I state the things in their chronological order, but the substance of the various interviews follows:
>
> Judge Sherman asked me if I wanted any advice from him on the matter. I said I would be glad to receive it. He told me that he thought it advisable from long experience to state all the reasons for and all the reasons against his testifying to the defendant and his people and let them decide.

Judge Sherman published in his "Recollections" this memorandum. (I have put in italics two sentences which have been thought significant.)

> James H. Vahey, during the trial of Charles L. Tucker for the murder of Mabel Page, entered the Judge's Lobby, after the adjournment of court, Judges Sherman and Sheldon, Sheriff John R. Fairbairn and Mr. Vahey, being present, the following conversation then took place.
>
> Mr. Vahey. Judge Sherman, you having had a large experience as Attorney General and as a Justice of this Court in capital trials, I want to ask your advice, as I have had little or no experience in such cases and am a good deal embarrassed.
>
> Judge Sherman. If I can properly advise you, I will.
>
> Mr. Vahey. Shall I put the prisoner on the witness stand?
>
> Judge Sherman. I do not think it would be proper for me to answer that question.
>
> Perhaps I can tell you what the rule and practice is among the best lawyers in such cases. *If the attorney believes his client innocent, put him on the witness stand without hesitation. If, however, he believes him guilty, never put him on the witness stand.* If the prisoner insists upon being a witness and the Attorney believes him guilty, the Attorney should say to him: 'I advise you not to testify, but as you have more interest in the case than I have, I shall not interfere.'

What do you say, Judge Sheldon?

Judge Sheldon. I fully concur in what you say about the practice among the best lawyers in such cases.

Mr. Vahey. I thank you, gentlemen, for advising me.

Some days after, Mr. Vahey again entered the Judge's Lobby and said:

After our interview the other evening, I told Tucker what you said to me concerning his being a witness.

After talking with him a long time, I told him to think it over carefully and then decide what to do.

Subsequently he told me that he had decided not to be a witness, and thereby he relieved me of a great responsibility, and I did not have to advise him.

Edgar J. Sherman,
H. N. Sheldon,
John R. Fairbairn.

I did not ask Mr. Vahey if he wanted me to advise him about Tucker's being a witness. The only conversation I ever had with him on that subject is stated in the above memorandum.

Edgar J. Sherman.

# UNCLE AMOS DREAMS A DREAM

## UNCLE AMOS DREAMS A DREAM

*Then answered Amos, and said . . . I was no prophet, neither was I a prophet's son; but I was a herdman, and a gatherer of sycamore fruit.*

YE who listen with skepticism to the voices of fancy, and gaze with disbelief upon visions at midnight; who scoff at the counsels of supernatural wisdom, and deride the sagacity of the dreamer of dreams; attend to the history of Amos Boorn of Vermont.

He was living, more than a hundred years ago, in the village of Manchester, in that State. It was a small place then, and it is a small place now, although known to thousands for its shady streets, its summer homes, its hotel, and its clouds of motorists and golfers. Motor-cars whir up and down its roads, and the click of the golf-ball is never still. A fair land, where the folk, with apparent lavishness, use marble for door-sills, curb-stones and sidewalks. A fair land among Green Mountains, which like many other mountains, are sometimes green, and sometimes blue or brown or white. And sometimes, like the fairy dog of Avalon, they are purple, when the shadows creep over them in the evening, and the whip-poor-wills begin. Across those mountains, but not far away, in another fair region, the President of the United States puts on a smock-frock when he goes to the milking, or jocund drives his team afield,—only to find, to his annoyance, that a man with a moving picture camera is there before him.

Early in 1812, there were living in Manchester a number of the Boorns: Amos, his brother Barney, his brother's wife, and the three (or four) children of Barney. The children whose names survive were Stephen, Jesse, and Sally. The sons and the daughter were all married, with families of their own. Sally Boorn for eighteen years had been married to Russell Colvin. There were at least two children; one named Lewis and one Rufus. Her husband, Russell, for a long time had been in a rather vague condition; he was "weak in his intellects." Although fond of his children, and given to carrying his little son Rufus about on his back, from place to place, he had an unfortunate habit of disappearing, and in one of these vanishing moods absented himself, in Rhode Island, for nearly a year. Again, on May 10, 1812, he disappeared utterly, and his neighbors saw him no more. For months and, at last, for years, nothing was known of Russell Colvin. The Boorns seemed to suggest that he was away on his wanderings again, and as they were not concerned about him, and as nobody else required his presence, nothing was done in the matter. War was being waged on land and sea and lake; the militiamen were training on the green, and Manchester did not think much about Colvin for six or seven years. Twice this length of time, by the way, intervened between the disappearance of Eugene Aram's victim, Daniel Clark, and the discovery of his bones.

But, by 1819, war had long been past; folk had time to reflect upon other things, and some of the Manches-